EASY AND FUN
KANJI
A Basic Guide to Learning Kanji

Author : Kiyomi Ogawa
English Editor : Orrin Cummins

IBC Publishing

Preface

I wrote this book as part of the Easy and Fun series after the hiragana and katakana books from that set. It took me quite a bit more time to put together than the previous two and there were a number of occasions where I wasn't quite sure how to proceed. I imagine that most people who are reading this book as part of their Japanese studies also feel that the kanji writing system is by far the hardest part of learning the Japanese language.

So why are kanji so difficult for both foreigners and native Japanese speakers like me? There are several reasons: the number of unique kanji is huge; they have complicated shapes; there are many ways to pronounce them; writing them is tricky.

Students often ask me how Japanese natives tackle the arduous task of memorizing kanji. The truth is that we learn the characters slowly over a period of many years, from elementary school (or even earlier) all the way through high school. Japanese children practice reading and writing kanji every day at school then work on them even more as part of their homework.

I think that many people who are learning Japanese as a secondary language are hesitant to study kanji because of this substantial time investment. That's why for this book I devised a faster method that differs from how Japanese natives approach kanji learning.

Since grade schools in Japan teach kanji in order of difficulty starting with the easiest, the characters needed for daily life (which are surprisingly difficult to memorize) are not learned until later, making that learning method unsuitable for foreigners who are staying in the country for a relatively short period of time.

This book instead presents the basic kanji alongside selected characters that are widely used in daily life while helping you become familiar with how they actually appear in the real world. I've also included some fun drawings that may serve as hints to help you remember the different kanji.

My hope is that this book will make memorizing kanji a more fun and enjoyable process for you.

Kiyomi Ogawa

カバーデザイン：岩目地英樹（コムデザイン）

まえがき

　この本はEasy and Funシリーズということで、ひらがな、かたかなに続き執筆しました。ひらがなとかたかなに比べると、漢字は時間もかかりましたし、色々と手こずる部分もありました。今これを読んでいる日本語学習者の方も、日本語の勉強の中で漢字が一番大変そうだと思っているでしょう。私も含め学習者はなぜ漢字を難しいと思うのでしょうか。膨大な数。複雑。発音がたくさんある。書き方が難しいなどなど様々な理由があると思います。

　そんなやっかいな漢字を、日本人はどうやって覚えるのかと生徒たちによく聞かれます。もちろん日本人も、そんなに簡単に覚えられません。小学校（あるいはその前から）から高校まで長い時間をかけて勉強するのです。毎日学校で読み書きを学び、家でもほとんど毎日のように漢字の宿題があります。

　学習者の中には、そんなに時間がかかるのなら勉強したくないと思う方もいると思います。

　そこでこの本では、日本人が漢字を覚えるのとは違った視点と方法で、早く覚えられるように工夫をしました。日本の学校の方法では、簡単な漢字から難しい漢字へと習っていくので、日常生活で必要な難しい漢字は覚えるのが後になってしまい、短期で日本に滞在する方には不向きといえます。本書では基本の漢字にあわせ、日常よく使われる漢字を選び、どのように生活で使われているかがわかるように工夫しました。また、漢字を覚えるためのヒントを楽しいイラストとともに記してあります。

　皆さんがこの本で、漢字を楽しく覚えることを願っています。

小川清美

How to Use This Book

First, review the rules for reading and writing kanji.

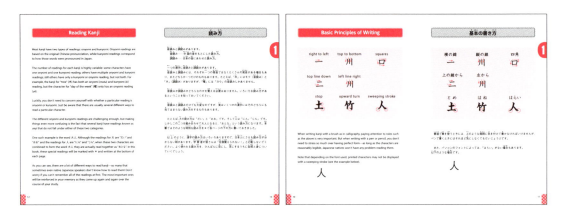

Kun'yomi readings are given in hiragana and *on'yomi* readings in katakana.

These are mnemonics to help you remember the characters. Some are true to the origin stories, while others I created to make learning the kanji easier.

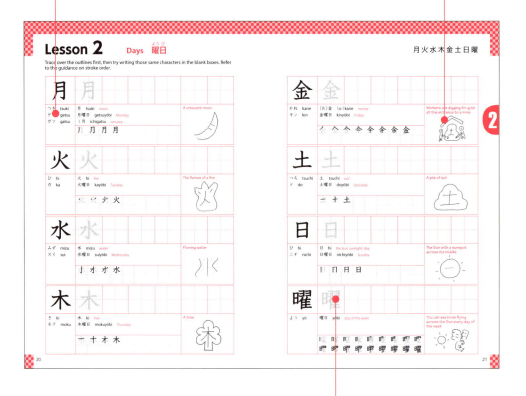

Using the stroke order as a guide, trace then write the characters.

Answers to the exercises can be found at the end of the book.

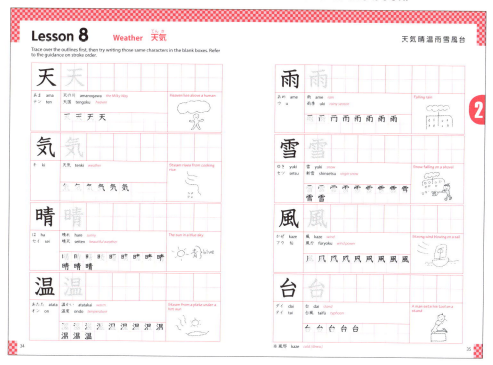

In this chapter, you will encounter some characters that you haven't learned yet. Just focus on their pronunciations and meanings.

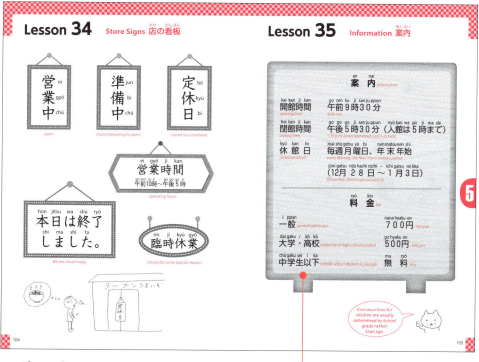

If you have a smartphone, snap some photos of these pages so you can refer to them while out and about.

Contents

Preface … 2
How to Use This Book … 4

Chapter 1 History and Usage 9
第一章　漢字の歴史と使われ方

The History of Kanji　漢字の歴史 … 10
Basic Principles of Writing　基本の書き方 … 12
Reading Kanji　読み方 … 14
Special Readings for Numbers　数字の特別な読み方 … 16

Chapter 2 Numbers, Pictograms, and Ideograms 19
第二章　数字、象形文字、会意文字

Lesson 1　Numbers　数字 … 20
Lesson 2　Days　曜日 … 22
Lesson 3　Nature　自然 … 24
Lesson 4　Sizes and Other Symbols　大きさ、記号など … 26
Lesson 5　Gender and Traits　性別、特性など … 28
Lesson 6　Body Parts and Left/Right　体、左右 … 30
Lesson 7　Combination Kanji　組み合わせた漢字 … 32
Lesson 8　Weather　天気 … 34
　● Exercise 1 … 36

Chapter 3 Radicals 39
第三章　部首

Lesson 9　The Water Radical　さんずい … 40
Lesson 10　The Roof Radical　うかんむり … 42

Lesson 11	The Word Radical　ごんべん	44
Lesson 12	The Thread Radical　糸(いと)へん	46
Lesson 13	The Person Radical　にんべん	48
Lesson 14	The Road Radical　しんにょう	50
Lesson 15	The Gate Radical and The Box Radical 門(もん)がまえ、国(くに)がまえ	52
● Exercise 2		54

Chapter 4　Kanji by Category 57
第四章(だい よん しょう)　種類別(しゅるいべつ)

Lesson 16	Information　情報(じょうほう)	58
Lesson 17	Addresses　住所(じゅうしょ)	60
Lesson 18	Direction　方角(ほうがく)	62
Lesson 19	School　学校(がっこう)	64
● Exercise 3		66
Lesson 20	Time　時間(じかん)	68
Lesson 21	Money　お金(かね)	70
Lesson 22	Family　家族(かぞく)	72
Lesson 23	Hobby　趣味(しゅみ)	74
● Exercise 4		76
Lesson 24	Food (1)　食(しょく)（1）	78
Lesson 25	Food (2)　食(しょく)（2）	80
Lesson 26	Drinks　飲(いん)	82
Lesson 27	Time　時(とき)	84
Lesson 28	Food (3)　食(しょく)（3）	86
● Exercise 5		88
Lesson 29	Buildings (1)　建物(たてもの)（1）	90
Lesson 30	Buildings (2)　建物(たてもの)（2）	92

Lesson 31	Transportation 交通	94
Lesson 32	Movement 動	96
Lesson 33	Seasons 季節	98
● Exercise 6		100

Chapter 5 Kanji in Daily Life (readings only) 103
第五章　日常生活で使われる漢字（読みだけ）

Lesson 34	Store Signs 店の看板	104
Lesson 35	information 案内	105
Lesson 36	Meal Tickets 食券	106
Lesson 37	Menu お品書き	107
Lesson 38	Station 駅	108
Lesson 39	Parking Lot 駐車場	109
Lesson 40	Remote Control リモコン	110
Lesson 41	Rice Cooker / Microwave 炊飯器／電子レンジ	111
Lesson 42	Washing Machine / Restroom 洗濯機／トイレ	112
Lesson 43	Hospital/Clinic 病院	113
Lesson 44	School 学校	114
Lesson 45	Ordering 注文	115

● Answers	116
● Index	119

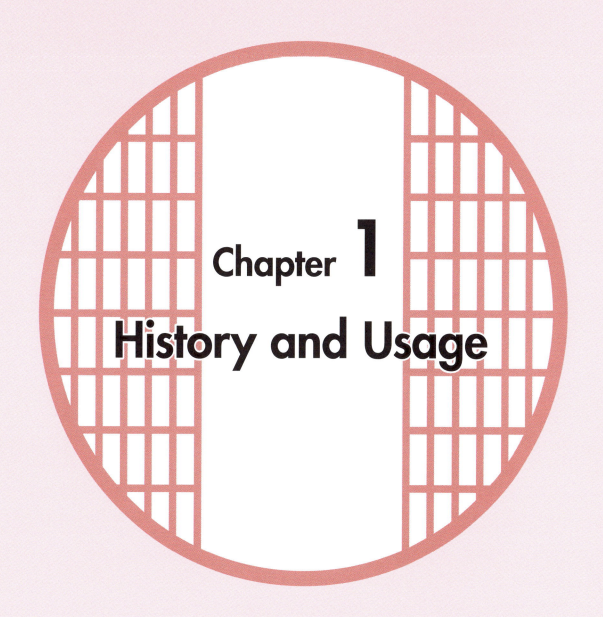

Chapter 1
History and Usage

第 一 章
だい いっしょう

漢字の歴史と使われ方
かんじ れきし つか かた

The History of Kanji

Kanji were first conceived in China around 2500 BC. It is said that the first character was created by imitating the footprint left by a bird walking on a sandy beach. The oldest extant kanji are the *kōkotsumoji* used during the Shang dynasty (1700–1046 BC). These pictograms— characters designed to resemble the appearance of objects—were carved into tortoise shells and animal bones used to converse with the gods. The Indus script and cuneiform are two examples of other writing systems that used pictograms.

New kanji were then developed to facilitate communication with other clans. Since these kanji were ideograms which represented ideas and concepts, people could understand each other even if they used different pronunciations. We are all familiar with at least one set of ideograms: the Arabic numerals used throughout the world. Eventually, phonograms representing sounds were also created and the number of kanji increased rapidly.

While the kanji writing system is generally believed to have been transmitted to Japan sometime after the end of the fourth century AD, some theories suggest that there were Japanese who could write kanji as early as the third century.

Because the meanings of many Chinese characters matched the meanings of Japanese words, a large number of kanji ended up with separate Chinese pronunciations (*on'yomi*) and Japanese pronunciations (*kun'yomi*). And in some cases, the meaning of a character in Japan actually diverged from its Chinese meaning. In addition, kanji unique to Japan were also developed; known as *kokuji*, these characters almost never have *on'yomi* pronunciations.

Between the formally established list of common characters (*jōyō kanji*) and the characters used in people's names, there are currently about 3,000 kanji in use in Japan.

漢字の歴史

　漢字は、B.C. 2500年頃、中国で作られました。砂浜を歩いた鳥の足跡を文字にしたのが最初だと言われています。現存している最古の漢字は殷の時代（B.C. 1700から1046年）に使用された甲骨文字です。甲骨文字は物の見た目を描く象形文字の一つで、象形文字には他にもインダス文字や楔形文字があります。甲骨文字は亀の甲羅や動物の骨に刻んで書かれ、神との対話のために使われました。

　その後、他部族との交信のために使う表意文字が作られました。表意文字は発音が違ってもお互いに分かり合える記号で、世界で使われるアラビア数字がその代表例です。また、音を表す表音文字も生まれ、漢字の数は飛躍的に増えました。

　日本にはA.D. 4世紀末ごろ伝来したと言われていますが、3世紀ごろに漢字を書くことができる日本人がいたという説もあるようです。

　中国の漢字の意味を日本語の言葉の意味にあてたため、中国の読み方（音読み）と別に日本語の読み方（訓読み）もできました。中には、意味そのものも中国のとは違うものもあります。さらに、日本にしかない漢字もできました。国字というものです。ほとんどの国字には音読みがありません。

　現在漢字は、常用漢字と人名用漢字を合わせて約3000字程度が日本で使われています。

Basic Principles of Writing

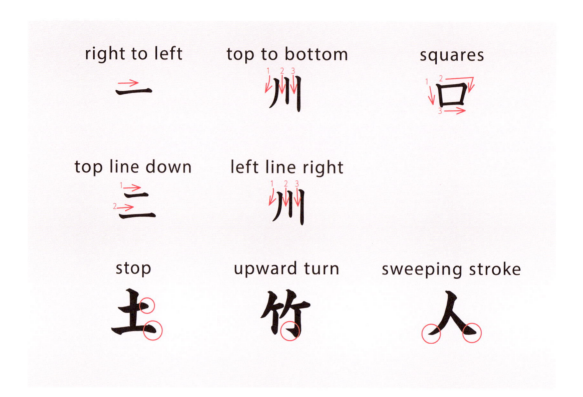

When writing kanji with a brush as in calligraphy, paying attention to rules such as the above is very important. But when writing with a pen or pencil, you don't need to stress so much over having perfect form—as long as the characters are reasonably legible, Japanese natives won't have any problem reading them.

Note that depending on the font used, printed characters may not be displayed with a sweeping stroke (see the example below).

基本の書き方

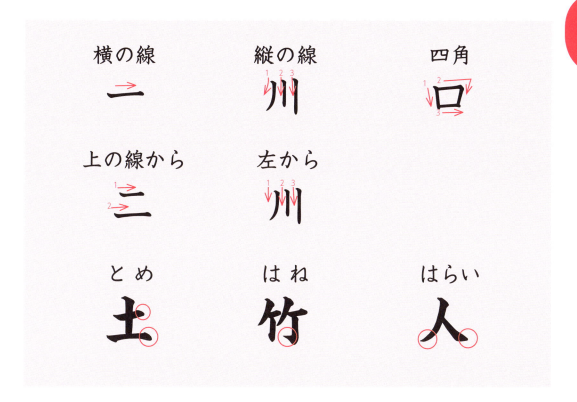

書道で筆を使うときには、上のような規則に気を付けて書かなければいけませんが、ペンで書くときにはそれほど気にしなくてもだいじょうぶです。

また、パソコンのフォントによっては、「はらい」がない場合もあります。以下のような場合です。

Reading Kanji

Most kanji have two types of readings: *on'yomi* and *kun'yomi*. On'yomi readings are based on the original Chinese pronunciation, while kun'yomi readings correspond to how those words were pronounced in Japan.

The number of readings for each kanji is highly variable: some characters have one on'yomi and one kun'yomi reading; others have multiple on'yomi and kun'yomi readings; still others have only a kun'yomi or on'yomi reading, but not both. For example, the kanji for "tree" (木) has both an on'yomi (*moku*) and kun'yomi (*ki*) reading, but the character for "day of the week" (曜) only has an on'yomi reading (*yō*).

Luckily, you don't need to concern yourself with whether a particular reading is on'yomi or kun'yomi. Just be aware that there are usually several different ways to read a particular character.

The different on'yomi and kun'yomi readings are challenging enough, but making things even more confusing is the fact that several kanji have readings known as *ateji* that do not fall under either of these two categories.

One such example is the word 大人. Although the readings for 大 are "だい" and "おお" and the readings for 人 are "にん" and "じん", when these two characters are combined to form the word 大人 they are actually read together as "おとな". In this book, these special readings will be marked with ※ and written at the bottom of each page.

As you can see, there are a lot of different ways to read kanji—so many that sometimes even native Japanese speakers don't know how to read them! Don't worry if you can't remember all of the readings at first. The most important ones will be reinforced in your memory as they come up again and again over the course of your study.

読み方

音読みと訓読みがあります。
　音読み……中国の音をもとにした読み方。
　訓読み……日本の音にあわせた読み方。

一つの漢字に音読みと訓読みがあります。
　音読みと訓読みには、それぞれ一つの発音ではなく、たくさんの発音がある場合もあり、またどちらか一つだけのものもあります。たとえば、「木」には「モク」（音読み）と「き」（訓読み）がありますが、「曜」には「ヨウ」の音読みしかありません。

　音読みか訓読みかどちらなのかを覚える必要はありません。いろいろな読み方があるということを知っておいてください。

　音読みと訓読みだけでも大変なのですが、実はいくつかの漢字には、そのどちらにも当てはまらない読み方をするものもあります。

　たとえば、「大」の読み方は「だい」と「おお」です。そして「人」は「にん」「じん」です。しかしこの二つを組み合わせて「大人」となると、「おとな」という読み方になります。本書ではそのような特別な読み方を※で各ページの下の方に書いておきました。

　以上のように、漢字の読み方はいろいろありますので、日本人にさえも読み方が分からない時があります。学習者の皆さんは「全部覚えられない！」と心配しないでください。よく使われる読み方を、ひんぱんに目にし、耳にするうちに自然と身についていくでしょう。

Special Readings for Numbers

Due to the many different counter suffixes, numbers have a wide variety of readings.

1. Things ···When counting between one and nine things, use 「つ」

一つ	hitotsu	one thing
二つ	futatsu	two things
三つ	mittsu	three things
四つ	yottsu	four things
五つ	itsutsu	five things
六つ	muttsu	six things
七つ	nanatsu	seven things
八つ	yattsu	eight things
九つ	kokonotsu	nine things
十	tō	ten things

2. People ···There are special expressions for "one person" and "two people." Starting with "three people," though, simply attach the suffix 「にん」 to the end of the number.

一人	hitori	one person
二人	futari	two people
三人	sannin	three people
四人	yonin	four people ···etc.

3. Dates ···The first ten days of a month as well as the fourteenth and twentieth days have special readings.

一日	tsuitachi	the first day of a month
二日	futsuka	the second day of a month
三日	mikka	the third day of a month
四日	yokka	the fourth day of a month
五日	itsuka	the fifth day of a month
六日	muika	the sixth day of a month
七日	nanoka	the seventh day of a month
八日	yōka	the eighth day of a month
九日	kokonoka	the ninth day of a month
十日	tōka	the tenth day of a month
十四日	jūyokka	the fourteenth day of a month
二十日	hatsuka	the twentieth day of a month

4. Ages ···The only age with a special reading is that for twenty years old: hatachi.

数字の特別な読み方

数字は助数詞によって発音が様々です。

1. 物…「つ」は物を数えるときに使います。

一つ	hitotsu
二つ	futatsu
三つ	mittsu
四つ	yottsu
五つ	itsusu
六つ	muttsu
七つ	nanatsu
八つ	yattsu
九つ	kokonotsu
十	tō

2. 人…1と2は特別な言い方があります。3以降は「人」をつけるだけで、音はすべて「にん」になります。

一人	hitori	
二人	futari	
三人	sannin	
四人	yonin	以下同

3. 日にち…1日から10日までと、14日、20日は特別な読み方があります。

一日	tsuitachi
二日	futsuka
三日	mikka
四日	yokka
五日	itsuka
六日	muika
七日	nanoka
八日	yōka
九日	kokonoka
十日	tōka
十四日	jūyokka
二十日	hatsuka

4. 年齢…20歳だけ特別に「はたち」と読みます。

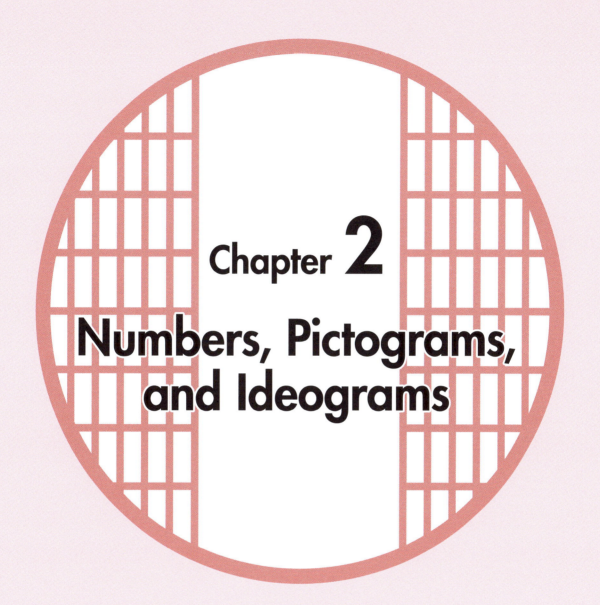

Chapter 2
Numbers, Pictograms, and Ideograms

第二章
数字、象形文字、会意文字

Lesson 1   Numbers 数字

Trace over the outlines first, then try writing those same characters in the blank boxes. Refer to the numbers and arrows for guidance on stroke order and direction.

| 一 | | | | | | | | **One stick** |
| ひと hito
 イチ ichi | 一つ hitotsu *one thing*
 一月 ichigatsu *January* | | | | | | | |

| 二 | | | | | | | | **Two sticks** |
| ふた futa
 ニ ni | 二つ futasu *two things*
 二月 nigatsu *February* | | | | | | | |

| 三 | | | | | | | | **Three sticks** |
| みっ mi
 サン san | 三つ mittsu *three things*
 三月 sangatsu *March* | | | | | | | |

| 四 | | | | | | | | **The four fingers of a hand** |
| よっ yo
 シ shi
 よん yon | 四つ yottsu *four things*
 四月 shigatsu *April*
 四枚 yonmai *four sheets (or similar thin objects)* | | | | | | | |

| 五 | | | | | | | | **Five sticks** |
| いつ itsu
 ゴ go | 五つ itsutsu *five things*
 五月 gogatsu *May* | | | | | | | |

一二三四五六七八九十

2

六							A mustached man in his sixties wearing a hat
むっ mu ロク roku	六つ muttsu *six things* 六月 rokugatsu *June*						

七							Touch your toes seven times to warm up
なな nana シチ shichi	七つ nanatsu *seven things* 七月 shichigatsu *July*						

八							A mustached man in his eighties
やっ ya ハチ hachi よう yō	八つ yattsu *eight things* 八月 hachigatsu *August* 八日 yōka *the eighth day of a month*						

九							Cats have nine lives
ここの kokono キュウ kyū ク ku	九つ kokonotsu *nine things* 九枚 kyūmai *nine sheets (or similar thin objects)* 九月 kugatsu *September*						

十							A bundle of ten sticks tied with a rope
とお tō ジュウ jū	十 tō *ten things* 十月 jūgatsu *October*						

Lesson 2

Days  曜日

Trace over the outlines first, then try writing those same characters in the blank boxes. Refer to the guidance on stroke order.

月

つき tsuki	月 tsuki *moon*
ゲツ getsu	月曜日 getsuyōbi *Monday*
ガツ gatsu	1月 ichigatsu *January*

月 月 月 月

A crescent moon

火

ひ hi	火 hi *fire*
カ ka	火曜日 kayōbi *Tuesday*

火 火 火 火

The flames of a fire

水

みず mizu	水 mizu *water*
スイ sui	水曜日 suiyōbi *Wednesday*

水 水 水 水

Flowing water

木

き ki	木 ki *tree*
モク moku	木曜日 mokuyōbi *Thursday*

木 木 木 木

A tree

月火水木金土日曜

金

かね kane
キン kin

(お)金 (o-)kane *money*
金曜日 kin'yōbi *Friday*

Workers are digging for gold at the entrance to a mine

土

つち tsuchi
ド do

土 tsuchi *soil*
土曜日 doyōbi *Saturday*

A pile of soil

日

ひ hi
ニチ nichi

日 hi *the Sun; sunlight; day*
日曜日 nichiyōbi *Sunday*

The Sun with a sunspot across its middle

曜

よう yō

曜日 yōbi *day of the week*

You can see birds flying across the Sun every day of the week

2

23

Lesson 3 Nature 自然

Trace over the outlines first, then try writing those same characters in the blank boxes. Refer to the guidance on stroke order.

山						
やま yama サン san	山田さん Yamada-san *a last name* 富士山 Fuji-san *Mount Fuji*					A mountain

川						
かわ kawa がわ gawa	山川さん Yamakawa-san *a last name* 小川さん Ogawa-san *a last name*					A river

田						
た ta だ da デン den	田んぼ tanbo *rice paddy* 山田さん Yamada-san *a last name* 水田 suiden *rice paddy flooded with water*					A rice paddy

井						
い i	井川さん Igawa-san *a last name* 井戸 ido *well*					A well

山川田井生竹羽立

2

生
- い i
- う u
- なま nama
- は ha
- セイ sei

生きる ikiru *to live*
生まれる umareru *to be born*
生魚 namazakana *raw fish*
生える haeru *to grow*
生年月日 seinengappi *birth date*

A plant growing

竹
- たけ take
- チク chiku

竹 take *bamboo*
竹林 chikurin *bamboo grove*

Two bamboo plants

羽
- はね hane
- ば ba
- ウ u

羽 hane *wing*
手羽 teba *chicken wing*
羽毛 umō *down (feather)*

Two wings

立
- た ta
- リツ ritsu

立つ tatsu *to stand*
公立 kōritsu *public*

A person standing

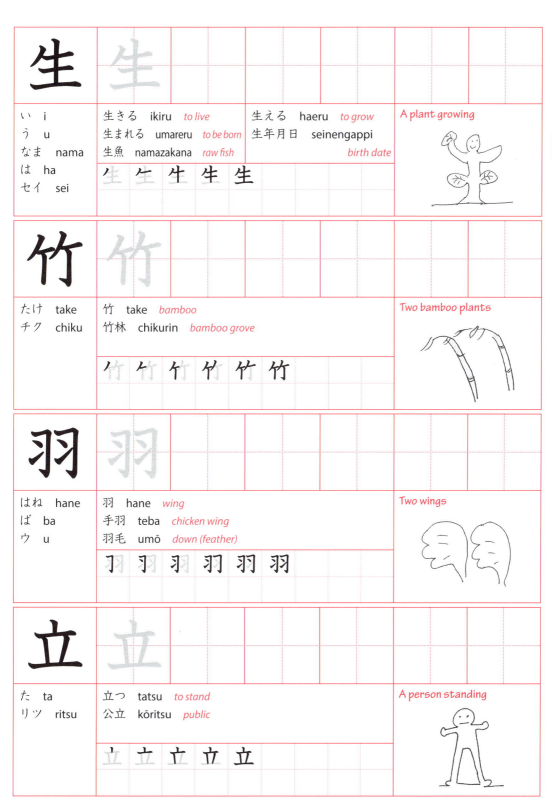

25

Lesson 4 Sizes and Other Symbols 大きさ、記号など

Trace over the outlines first, then try writing those same characters in the blank boxes. Refer to the guidance on stroke order.

大

おお ō
ダイ dai

大きい ōkii *big, large*
大学 daigaku *university*

A person with arms and legs spread wide

中

なか naka
チュウ chū

田中さん Tanaka-san *a last name*
中学 chūgaku *middle school*

The middle of a top

小

ちい chii
ショウ shō

小さい chiisai *small, little*
小学 shōgaku *elementary school*

Scattered small branches

人

ひと hito
ジン jin

人 hito *person*
日本人 Nihonjin *a Japanese person*

A human

※ 大人 otona *adult*

大中小人上下休入

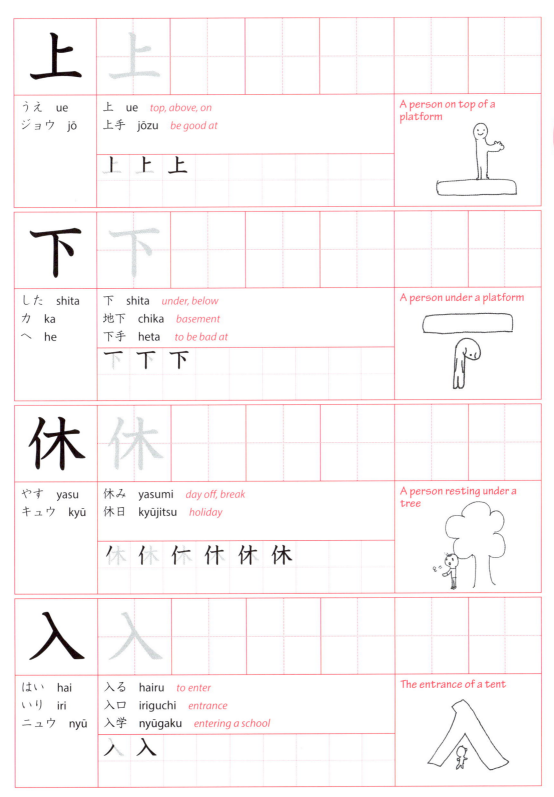

| 上 | うえ ue
ジョウ jō | 上 ue *top, above, on*
上手 jōzu *be good at* | A person on top of a platform |

②

| 下 | した shita
カ ka
ヘ he | 下 shita *under, below*
地下 chika *basement*
下手 heta *to be bad at* | A person under a platform |

| 休 | やす yasu
キュウ kyū | 休み yasumi *day off, break*
休日 kyūjitsu *holiday* | A person resting under a tree |

| 入 | はい hai
いり iri
ニュウ nyū | 入る hairu *to enter*
入口 iriguchi *entrance*
入学 nyūgaku *entering a school* | The entrance of a tent |

Lesson 5   Gender and Traits   性別、特性など
せいべつ　とくせい

Trace over the outlines first, then try writing those same characters in the blank boxes. Refer to the guidance on stroke order.

力

ちから　chikara
リキ　riki

力　chikara　*power*
人力車　jinrikisha　*rickshaw*

A muscular arm

子

こ　ko
シ　shi

男の子　otokonoko　*boy*
男子　danshi　*boy (used at school)*

A small child with a big head

女

おんな　onna
ジョ　jo

女の子　onnanoko　*girl*
女子　joshi　*girl (used at school)*

A sitting woman

男

おとこ　otoko
ダン　dan

男の人　otokonohito　*man*
男性　dansei　*male*

Rice paddy + muscular arm = a man working in a rice paddy

力子女男好心性学

2

好
- す su
- この kono
- コウ kō

好き suki *like*
お好み焼き okonomiyaki *name of a Japanese dish*
大好物 daikōbutsu *favorite food*

A child likes its mother (a woman)

心
- こころ kokoro
- シン shin

心 kokoro *heart*
心配 shinpai *worry*

A human heart

性
- せい sei
- ショウ shō

女性 josei *female*
気性 kishō *temper*

The nature of a thing develops in its heart as it grows

学
- まな mana
- ガク gaku

学ぶ manabu *to learn*
学生 gakusei *student*

Giving knowledge to a child in a school building

Lesson 6 Body Parts and Left/Right 体、左右
からだ　さゆう

Trace over the outlines first, then try writing those same characters in the blank boxes. Refer to the guidance on stroke order.

目

め	me
モク	moku

目 me *eye*
科目 kamoku *course, subject*

An eye

口

くち	kuchi
コウ	kō

口 kuchi *mouth*
人口 jinkō *population*

A mouth

耳

みみ	mimi
ジ	ji

耳 mimi *ear*
耳鼻科 jibika *ear, nose, and throat (doctor, clinic, etc.)*

An ear

出

で	de
シュツ	shutsu

出る deru *to go out*
出発 shuppatsu *departure*

A foot is exiting from a door

目口耳出手見右左

手			
て te シュ shu	手 te *hand* 手工芸 shukōgei *handicraft*		A hand

見			
み mi ケン ken	見る miru *to look, see, watch* 見学 kengaku *a field trip or tour of a facility*		An eye on a human

右			
みぎ migi ウ u ユウ yū	右手 migite *right hand* 右折 usetsu *right turn* 座右 zayū *close at hand*		Right hand picking up a bowl

左			
ひだり hidari サ sa	左手 hidarite *left hand* 左右 sayū *left and right*		Left hand working on a craft

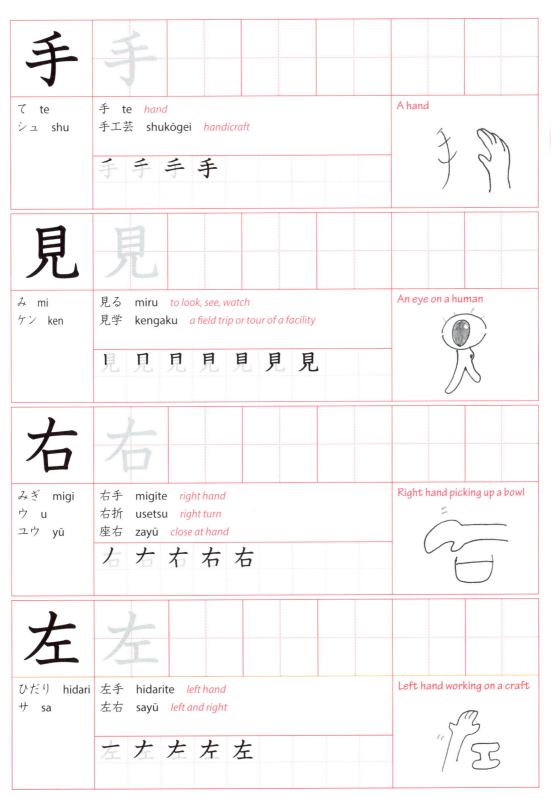

2

31

Lesson 7 Combination Kanji 組み合わせた漢字

Trace over the outlines first, then try writing those same characters in the blank boxes. Refer to the guidance on stroke order.

林
はやし hayashi
リン rin

林 hayashi — *grove*
林さん Hayashi-san — *a last name*
林道 rindō — *woodland path*

Two trees

森
もり mori
シン shin

森 mori — *forest*
大森さん Ōmori-san — *a last name*
森林 shinrin — *woodlands*

Three trees

明
あか aka
メイ mei

明るい akarui — *bright*
証明書 shōmeisho — *certificate*

Sun + moon = bright

暗
くら kura
アン an

暗い kurai — *dark*
暗号 angō — *code*

A person stands in the shade to avoid two suns

32 ※ 明日 ashita / asu *tomorrow*

林森明暗禁止煙災

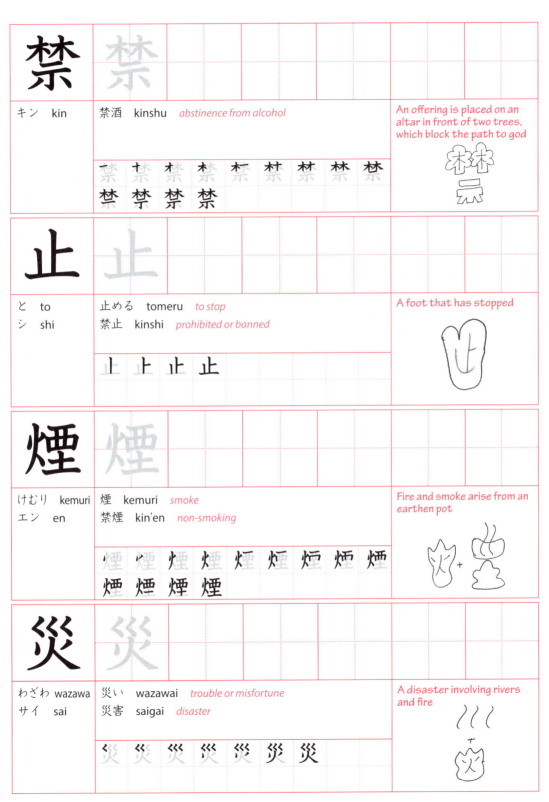

禁
キン kin
禁酒 kinshu *abstinence from alcohol*

An offering is placed on an altar in front of two trees, which block the path to god

止
と to
シ shi
止める tomeru *to stop*
禁止 kinshi *prohibited or banned*

A foot that has stopped

煙
けむり kemuri
エン en
煙 kemuri *smoke*
禁煙 kin'en *non-smoking*

Fire and smoke arise from an earthen pot

災
わざわ wazawa
サイ sai
災い wazawai *trouble or misfortune*
災害 saigai *disaster*

A disaster involving rivers and fire

33

Lesson 8   Weather 天気(てんき)

Trace over the outlines first, then try writing those same characters in the blank boxes. Refer to the guidance on stroke order.

天
- あま ama
- テン ten
- 天の川 amanogawa — *the Milky Way*
- 天国 tengoku — *heaven*

Heaven lies above a human

気
- キ ki
- 天気 tenki — *weather*

Steam rises from cooking rice

晴
- は ha
- セイ sei
- 晴れ hare — *sunny*
- 晴天 seiten — *beautiful weather*

The sun in a blue sky — 青 } blue

温
- あたた atata
- オン on
- 温かい atatakai — *warm*
- 温度 ondo — *temperature*

Steam from a plate under a hot sun

天気晴温雨雪風台

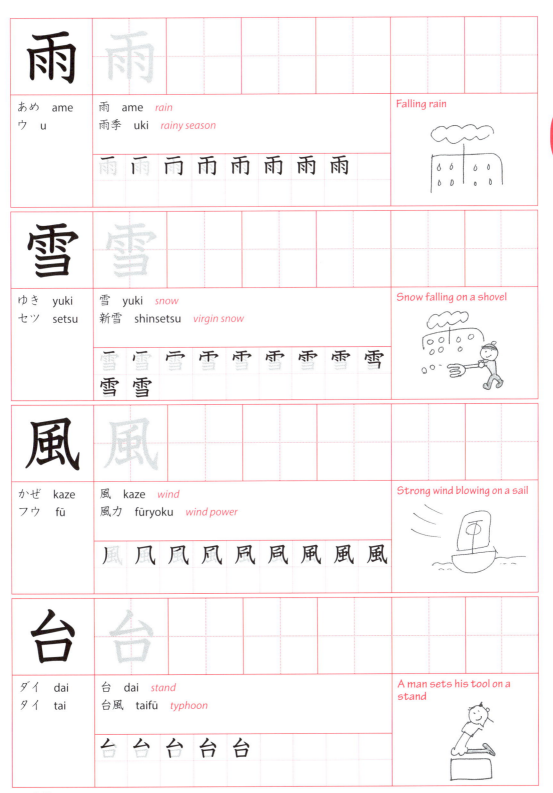

※ 風邪　kaze　*cold (illness)*

Exercise 1

(Answers: p.116)

I   Match the following kanji to their meanings.

金 •   • like

生 •   • rain

休 •   • gold

好 •   • rest

雨 •   • raw

II Choose the correct kanji from the right side and write them in the spaces provided.

entrance	(　) 口	入・人
right hand	(　) 手	右・左
no smoking	(　) 煙	禁・林
to see	(　) る	目・見

Ⅲ　Practice reading the following sentences aloud.

1　一月一日は休みです。
2　水を二はいおねがいします。
3　あの大きい人は、山田さんです。
4　この男の子は、その女の子が好きです。
5　森の中は暗いです。
6　明日の天気は、晴れでしょう。
7　左手を見てください。
8　ここは、立ち入り禁止です。
9　日本人は、目が小さいです。
10　女性の心はふくざつです。

Ⅳ　Write the following words in kanji.

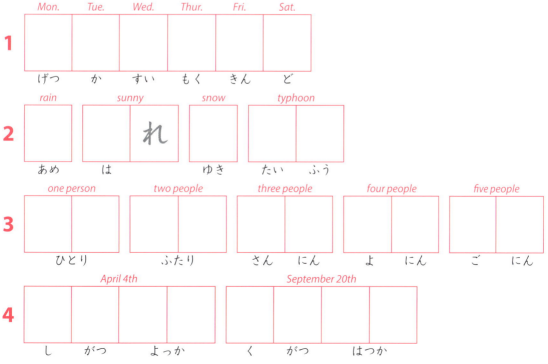

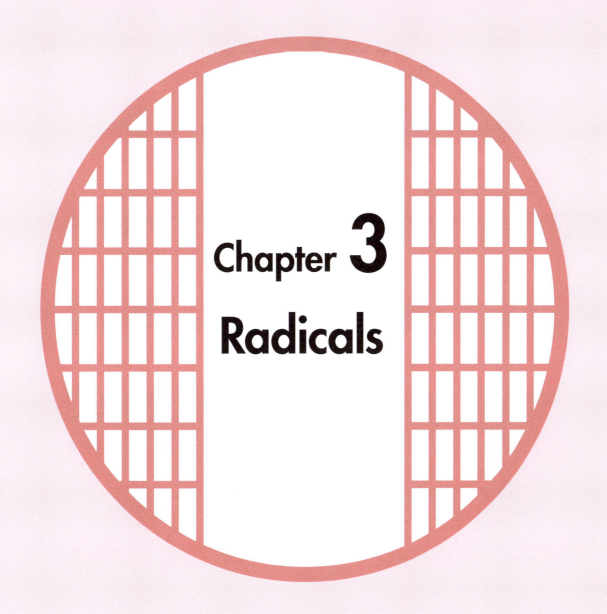

Chapter 3
Radicals

だい さん しょう
第 三 章

ぶ しゅ
部 首

Lesson 9   The Water Radical   さんずい

Trace over the outlines first, then try writing those same characters in the blank boxes. Refer to the guidance on stroke order.

汁

しる shiru
ジュウ jū

みそ汁   miso shiru   *miso soup*
一汁一菜   ichijūissai   *a bowl of soup plus one dish; a simple meal*

Soup containing ten vegetables

海

うみ umi
カイ kai

海 umi   *sea*
日本海   Nihonkai   *Sea of Japan*

Going to the beach every day

池

いけ ike
チ chi

池 ike   *pond*
遊園地   yūenchi   *amusement park*

A snake emerges from water

湖

みずうみ mizuumi
コ ko

湖 mizuumi   *lake*
山中湖   Yamanaka-ko   *Lake Yamanaka*

A boat drifts on a lake under the moon

汁海池湖泣注汗活

| 泣 | な na
キュウ kyū | 泣く naku *to cry*
号泣 gōkyū *wailing or crying aloud* | A standing boy is crying |

| 注 | そそ soso
チュウ chū | 注ぐ sosogu *to pour*
注意 chūi *attention* | A woman pours sake for her husband |

| 汗 | あせ ase
カン kan | 汗 ase *sweat*
制汗剤 seikanzai *deodorant* | A dry man got sweaty |

| 活 | カツ katsu | 生活 seikatsu *lifestyle, living life* | It's hard to live by catching raindrops with your tongue |

Lesson 10 The Roof Radical うかんむり

Trace over the outlines first, then try writing those same characters in the blank boxes. Refer to the guidance on stroke order.

家

いえ ie	家 ie *house*
うち uchi	家 uchi *home*
や ya	我が家 wagaya *our house; our family*
カ ka	家族 kazoku *family*
ケ ke	小川家 Ogawa-ke *the Ogawa family*

A pig in a house

安

やす yasu	安い yasui *inexpensive or cheap*
アン an	安心 anshin *relief*

A woman is relieved to be at home

客

キャク kyaku	お客さん o-kyaku-san *guest or customer*

Welcoming a guest into the home

室

しつ shitsu	客室 kyakushitsu *guest room*

A person sits on the earthen floor of a room

家安客室害守容定

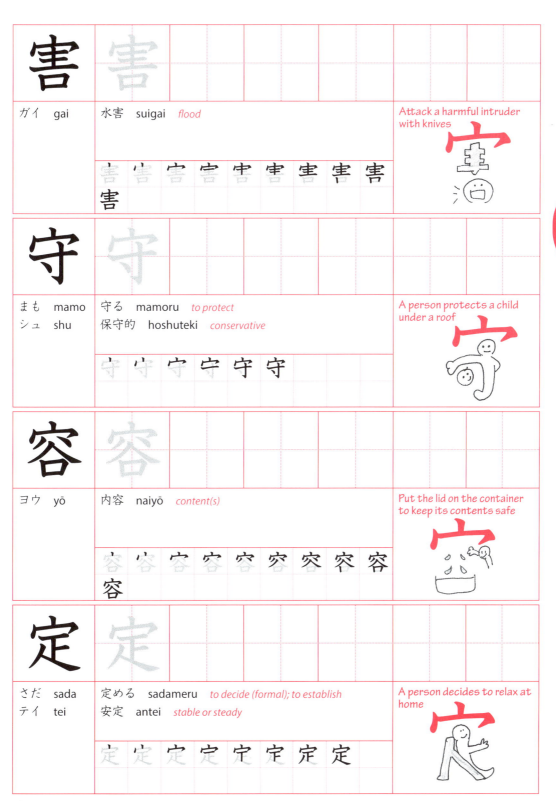

害	ガイ gai	水害 suigai *flood*	Attack a harmful intruder with knives
守	まも mamo / シュ shu	守る mamoru *to protect* 保守的 hoshuteki *conservative*	A person protects a child under a roof
容	ヨウ yō	内容 naiyō *content(s)*	Put the lid on the container to keep its contents safe
定	さだ sada / テイ tei	定める sadameru *to decide (formal); to establish* 安定 antei *stable or steady*	A person decides to relax at home

3

43

Lesson 11 The Word Radical ごんべん

Trace over the outlines first, then try writing those same characters in the blank boxes. Refer to the guidance on stroke order.

言
- い i
- ゲン gen
- 言う iu — *to say*
- 言語 gengo — *language*

Putting a lid on a talkative person

話
- はな hana
- ワ wa
- 話す hanasu — *to talk; to speak*
- 会話 kaiwa — *conversation*

Speaking a thousand words

言 + 千 = 1000 + 口

語
- かた kata
- ゴ go
- 語る kataru — *to talk; to tell*
- 日本語 Nihongo — *Japanese language*

Five mouths are speaking

言 + 五 = 5 + 口

訳
- わけ wake
- ヤク yaku
- 訳 wake — *reason*
- 通訳 tsūyaku — *interpreting*

A person stands and states a reason

44

言 話 語 訳 談 読 記 計

談
ダン　dan

冗談　jōdan　*joke*

Did I tell you the joke about the two fires?

読
よ　yo
ドク　doku

読む　yomu　*to read*
音読　ondoku　*reading aloud*

People's comments are sold in books then read
言 読) to sell

記
しる　shiru
キ　ki

記す　shirusu　*to jot down*
日記　nikki　*journal or diary*

Taking notes about oneself

計
はか　haka
ケイ　kei

計る　hakaru　*to measure*
合計　gōkei　*total*

Say the total aloud ten times
言 十 =10

3

45

Lesson 12 The Thread Radical 糸へん

Trace over the outlines first, then try writing those same characters in the blank boxes. Refer to the guidance on stroke order.

糸

いと ito

糸 ito *thread*
毛糸 keito *yarn*

A spool of thread

綿

わた wata
メン men

綿あめ wataame *cotton candy*
綿花 menka *raw cotton*

Cotton is a cloth made from white thread

絹

きぬ kinu
ケン ken

絹 kinu *silk*
正絹 shōken *pure silk*

Beautiful silk thread comes from a cocoon at night

結

むす musu
ゆう yū
ケツ ketsu

結ぶ musubu *to tie*
結城 yūki *a place or a last name*
結婚 kekkon *marriage*

A gift tied with thread in the shape of a bow

糸 綿 絹 結 紙 約 終 給

紙
かみ kami
シ shi

紙 kami *paper*
用紙 yōshi *a form*

Organize papers by last name and bind them with a string

約
ヤク yaku

予約 yoyaku *reservation*
約束 yakusoku *promise*

A person tying string to a tree to remember a promise

3

終
お o
シュウ shū

終わる owaru *to finish*
終える oeru *to stop*
終了 shūryō *end*

The food we hung up with thread for the winter has run out

給
たま tama
キュウ kyū

給う tamau *to provide*
給料 kyūryō *salary*

Remove the lid and the container will provide you with string

Lesson 13   The Person Radical   にんべん

Trace over the outlines first, then try writing those same characters in the blank boxes. Refer to the guidance on stroke order.

使
つか tsuka
シ shi

使う　tsukau　*to use*
大使　taishi　*ambassador*

An ambassador with a big hat brings a letter

作
つく tsuku
サク saku

作る　tsukuru　*to make*
作品　sakuhin　*a work product (especially artwork)*

A person making something from wood

何
なに nani
なん nan

何　nani　*what*
何時　nanji　*what time*

A man is asking "What?"

住
す su
ジュウ jū

住む　sumu　*to live*
住所　jūsho　*address*

A man lighting a candle where he lives

使作何住価値代付

価

あたい　atai
カ　ka

価　atai　*value*
定価　teika　*fixed price*

A person heads west to find valuable treasure

値

ね　ne
チ　chi

安値　yasune　*low price*
価値　kachi　*value*

A soothsayer tells a man his future for a price

代

か　ka
ダイ　dai

代わる　kawaru　*to substitute*
代金　daikin　*a charge or fee*

People take turns working on a sunny day

付

つ　tsu
フ　fu

付ける　tsukeru　*to put on; to apply*
給付　kyūfu　*provision*

A person applying paint to a sign

49

Lesson 14 The Road Radical しんにょう

Trace over the outlines first, then try writing those same characters in the blank boxes. Refer to the guidance on stroke order.

道
- みち michi
- ドウ dō

さか道 sakamichi *hill*
車道 shadō *roadway*

A person with a long neck is on the road

近
- ちか chika
- キン kin

近い chikai *near*
近所 kinjo *neighborhood*

An old woman with a cane passes on the road nearby

遠
- とお tō
- エン en

遠い tōi *far*
遠足 ensoku *field trip*

A little prince who has a hat on his head goes on a trip down the road

迷
- まよ mayo
- メイ mei

迷う mayou *to get lost*
迷信 meishin *superstition*

There are many ways to go and get lost

道近遠迷送迎返週

送
おく oku
ソウ sō

送る okuru — to send (an object)
転送する tensō suru — to forward or transfer

Sending an offering on the road to heaven

迎
むか muka
ゲイ gei

迎える mukaeru — to welcome, to pick someone up
送迎バス sōgeibasu — shuttle bus

A mother picks up her child from the side of the road

返
かえ kae
ヘン hen

返す kaesu — to return
返信する henshin suru — to reply

The road is blocked and he has to return

週
シュウ shū

今週 konshū — this week

This week I walked around a cul-de-sac

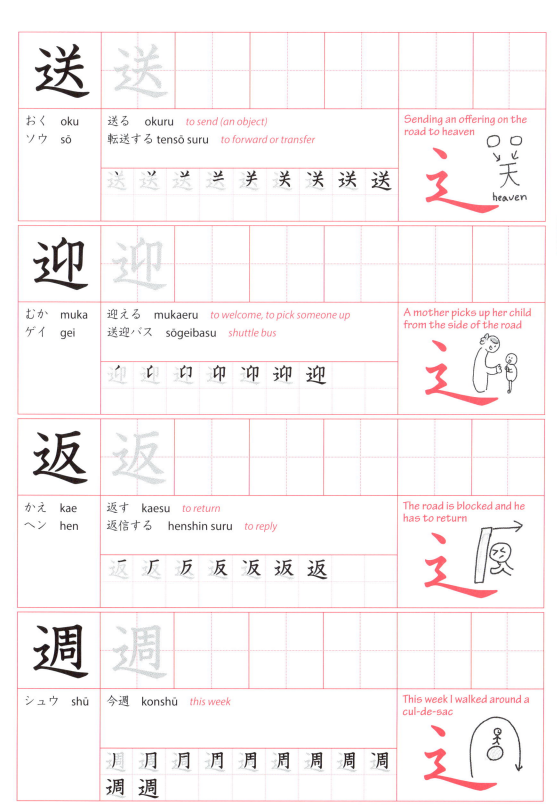

3

51

Lesson 15　The Gate Radical 門がまえ(もん)

Trace over the outlines first, then try writing those same characters in the blank boxes. Refer to the guidance on stroke order.

門
- かど　kado
- モン　mon

門出　kadode　*departure, new life*
門　mon　*gate*

A gate

開
- あ　a
- カイ　kai

開ける　akeru　*to open*
開店　kaiten　*open (a store)*

A bar on the gate is open

閉
- し　shi
- ヘイ　hei

閉める　shimeru　*to close*
閉店　heiten　*closed (a store)*

A bar on the gate is closed

聞
- き　ki
- ブン　bun

聞く　kiku　*to listen*
新聞　shinbun　*newspaper*

Listening to news happening outside the gate

The Box Radical 国がまえ

門開閉聞国図回園

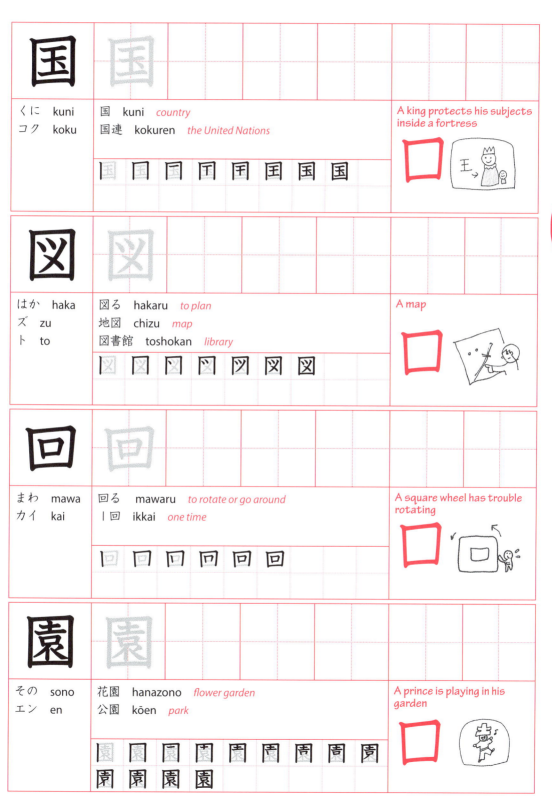

Exercise 2

(Answers: p.116)

I   Match the following kanji to their meanings.

<table>
<tr><td>海</td><td>•</td><td>•</td><td>what</td></tr>
<tr><td>客</td><td>•</td><td>•</td><td>guest</td></tr>
<tr><td>読</td><td>•</td><td>•</td><td>sea</td></tr>
<tr><td>終</td><td>•</td><td>•</td><td>read</td></tr>
<tr><td>何</td><td>•</td><td>•</td><td>finish</td></tr>
</table>

II Choose the correct kanji from the right side and write them in the spaces provided.

relief	（　）心	安・守
diary / journal	日（　）	語・記
one time	一（　）	回・国
fixed price	定（　）	四・価

Ⅲ　Practice reading the following sentences aloud.

1　一週間に二回、ジムに行きます。
2　注意してください。
3　湖は池より大きいです。
4　この紙に地図を書きましょうか。
5　門を開けてください。
6　結婚しています。
7　その冗談は何回も聞きましたよ。
8　ここの近くに住んでいます。
9　道に迷いました。
10　ようち園は閉まっています。

Ⅳ　Write the following words in kanji.

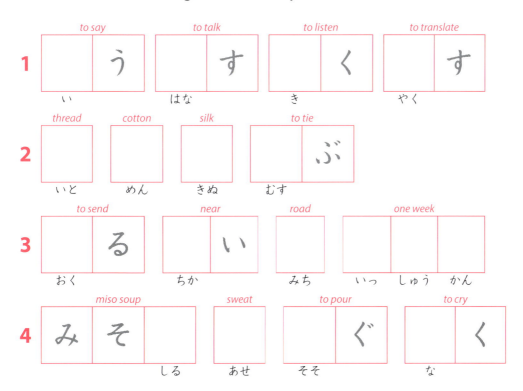

Lesson 16   Information 情報(じょうほう)

Trace over the outlines first, then try writing those same characters in the blank boxes. Refer to the guidance on stroke order.

氏
シ shi

氏 shi — *last name*
田中氏 Tanaka-shi — *Mr. Tanaka (used in writing)*

Married couples have the same last name

名
な na
メイ mei

名前 namae — *name*
名刺 meishi — *business card*
氏名 shimei — *full name*

Say your name at night because no one can recognize you in the dark

才
サイ sai

何才 nansai — *how old, what age*
天才 tensai — *genius*

The genius boy is dancing on his birthday

所
ところ tokoro
ショ sho

所 tokoro — *place*
事務所 jimusho — *office*

The bullseye is the place to aim at

58

氏名才所電番号職

| 電 | デン den | 電気　denki　*electricity* | Rain and lightning over a rice paddy |

| 番 | バン ban | 番　ban　*guard*
一番　ichiban　*number one* | A scarecrow is guarding a rice paddy |

| 号 | ゴウ gō | 号泣　gōkyū　*to wail*
番号　bangō　*number* | A woman is wailing because her number wasn't called |

| 職 | ショク shoku | 職業　shokugyō　*occupation* | Hearing the sound of someone working |

4

Lesson 17　　Addresses　住所 (じゅうしょ)

Trace over the outlines first, then try writing those same characters in the blank boxes. Refer to the guidance on stroke order.

県

ケン　ken

県　ken　*prefecture*

There is a guard watching each prefecture

市

いち　ichi
シ　shi

市場　ichiba　*market*
市　shi　*city*

A town market

区

ク　ku

区　ku　*ward*

Draw lines on a map to create wards

町

まち　machi
チョウ　chō

町　machi　*town*
町長　chōchō　*town mayor*

Rice paddies on the edge of town are marked with nails

県市区町州京府都

州
- す su
- シュウ shū
- 中州 nakasu — *a sandbank in a river*
- 州 shū — *state*

States are often divided by rivers

京
- キョウ kyō
- 京都府 Kyōto-fu — *Kyoto metropolitan prefecture*

People from Kyōto have small mouths

府
- フ fu
- 政府 seifu — *government*

Handling important work in a government building

都
- みやこ miyako
- ト to
- 都 miyako — *capital*
- 東京都 Tōkyō-to — *the capital city of Tokyo*

You can "B" any person you want in the capital

4

61

Lesson 18 Direction 方角(ほうがく)

Trace over the outlines first, then try writing those same characters in the blank boxes. Refer to the guidance on stroke order.

東

ひがし higashi トウ tō	東 higashi *east* 関東地方 Kantō chihō *a region in eastern Japan*

An arrow points toward the sun as it rises in the east

西

にし nishi セイ sei サイ sai	西 nishi *west* 西洋 seiyō *Western (culture, country, etc.)* 関西地方 Kansai chihō *a region in western Japan*

Birds live in baskets out West

南

みなみ minami ナン nan	南 minami *south* 東南アジア Tōnan Ajia *Southeast Asia*

Southern farmers make a lot of yen (¥) because plants grow well there

北

きた kita ホク hoku	北 kita *north* 東北地方 Tōhoku chihō *a region in northern Japan*

Two people sitting back to back because their relationship is cold like northern weather

※ 東西南北 Tōzainanboku *cardinal directions*

東西南北関地方角

Lesson 19   School   学校(がっこう)

Trace over the outlines first, then try writing those same characters in the blank boxes. Refer to the guidance on stroke order.

校

コウ kō

学校 gakkō *school*

Father went to school in a wooden building

先

さき saki
セン sen

お先に o-saki ni *I'll go ahead (of you)*
先生 sensei *teacher*

The warrior with the stick ran ahead of me

年

とし toshi
ネン nen

年上 toshiue *someone who is older (relative to someone else)*
一年生 ichinensei *first-grade student*

Once a year people harvest rice using a sickle

高

たか taka
コウ kō

高い takai *high or expensive*
高校生 kōkōsei *high-school student*

A tall building

校先年高教科授業

教

おし oshi
キョウ kyō

教える oshieru *to teach*
教科 kyōka *general subject in school*

A teacher shovels knowledge into a kid's head like soil

科

カ ka

科目 kamoku *specific course in school*
科学 kagaku *science*

I'm taking a course on how to measure rice

4

授

さず sazu
ジュ ju

授ける sazukeru *to give or grant*
授業 jugyō *class*

We give and receive things with our hands

業

ギョウ gyō

業務 gyōmu *business, duties*
開業 kaigyō *begin a business*

A person doing a lot of work

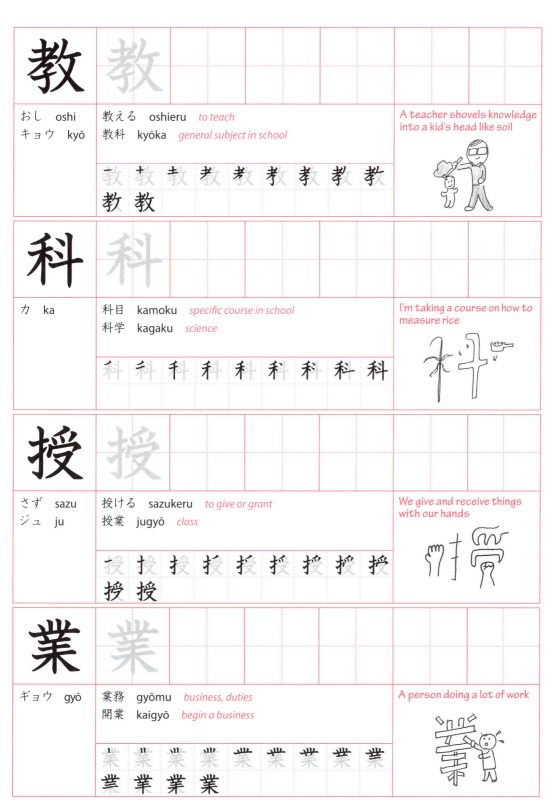

65

Exercise 3

(Answers: p.117)

I Match the following kanji to their meanings.

町　•　　　　•　south

南　•　　　　•　ward

高　•　　　　•　ahead

先　•　　　　•　town

区　•　　　　•　high

II Choose the correct kanji from the right side and write them in the spaces provided.

Tokyo　　　（　）京　　　東・西

class　　　（　）業　　　科・授

school　　　学（　）　　　村・校

address　　　住（　）　　　所・県

Ⅲ　Practice reading the following sentences aloud.

1　何才ですか。
2　学校の授業は、むずかしいです。
3　わたしは、高校二年生です。
4　好きな教科は何ですか。
5　氏名、職業、電話番号を記入する。
6　大阪府は関西地方にあります。
7　東京都は関東地方にあります。
8　京都に十年住んでいます。
9　アメリカの州で、テキサス州は二番目に大きいです。
10　日本には、県があります。

Ⅳ　Write the following words in kanji.

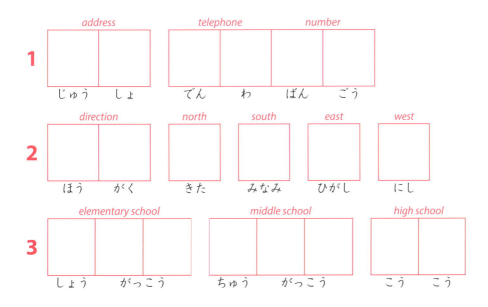

Lesson 20　　Time　時間(じかん)

Trace over the outlines first, then try writing those same characters in the blank boxes. Refer to the guidance on stroke order.

午

ゴ　go

午前　gozen　*morning*

The farmer takes a break at 10 in the morning

前

まえ　mae
ゼン　zen

前　mae　*front, ahead*
前回　zenkai　*the last time or previous time*

Cut the rope so that the boat can proceed ahead

後

うし　ushi
ゴ　go

後ろ　ushiro　*back, behind*
午後　gogo　*afternoon*

Two kids follow behind their mother down the road by holding strings

時

とき　toki
ジ　ji

時　toki　*time*
一時　ichiji　*one o'clock*

The sun's position tells the temple monk when it is time to ring the bell

※ 時計　tokei　*clock*

午前後時間分仕事

間
あいだ aida
カン kan

間 aida *between or among*
時間 jikan *time, hour*

The sun rises between the doors of the gate

分
フン fun
ブン bun

２分 nifun *two minutes*
半分 hanbun *half*

Use a knife to cut a cake in half

4

仕
つか tsuka
シ shi

仕える tsukaeru *to serve*
使用する shiyō suru *to use*

A lady and her servant

事
こと koto
ジ ji

こと koto *thing*
用事 yōji *errand*

This sacred wand is used to bless things

69

Lesson 21 Money お金(かね)

Trace over the outlines first, then try writing those same characters in the blank boxes. Refer to the guidance on stroke order.

円

まる maru
エン en

円い marui *circular or round*
円 en *yen (Japanese currency)*

A coin

料

りょう ryō

料金 ryōkin *fee*
食料 shokuryō *food*

Measure the rice to determine the purchase fee

無

な na
ム mu

無い nai *nonexistent or absent (inanimate things only)*
無料 muryō *free of charge*

Empty a box of chocolates by turning it over

有

あ a
ユウ yū

有る aru *existent or present (inanimate things only)*
有料 yūryō *not free of charge*

The moon exists under the cloud

円料無億有万千百

億

オク　oku

億　oku　*one hundred million*

There are one hundred million people standing on the sun's heart

万

マン　man

万　man　*ten thousand*

The bills in the bag are worth ten thousand yen each

千

ち　chi
セン　sen

千代田区　Chiyoda-ku　*a special ward of Tokyo*
千円　sen en　*one thousand yen*

Ten sticks tied with a string cost one thousand yen

百

ヒャク　hyaku

百円　hyaku en　*one hundred yen*

It took the spaceship one hundred days to reach the sun

4

Lesson 22 Family 家族(かぞく)

Trace over the outlines first, then try writing those same characters in the blank boxes. Refer to the guidance on stroke order.

母
- かあ kā
- はは haha
- ボ bo

お母さん okāsan *mother*
母 haha *my mother*
母子 boshi *mother and child*

A mother has two children

父
- とう tō
- ちち chichi
- フ fu

お父さん otōsan *father*
父 chichi *my father*
父子 fushi *father and child*

An angry father stands with hands on hips

兄
- にい nii
- あに ani
- キョウ kyō

お兄さん oniisan *older brother*
兄 ani *my older brother*
兄弟 kyōdai *siblings*

The older brother speaks up as a representative of his family

姉
- ねえ nē
- あね ane
- シ shi

お姉さん onēsan *older sister*
姉 ane *my older sister*
姉妹 shimai *sisters*

The older sister is dressed in a kimono for her wedding

母父兄姉妹弟私族

妹
いもうと imōto
マイ mai

妹 imōto *younger sister*
義妹 gimai *sister-in-law *used in writing*
(giri no imōto is the colloquial way)

My younger sister always wears a dress

弟
おとうと otōto
ダイ dai
テイ tei

弟 otōto *younger brother*
師弟 shitei *master and pupil*

The end of the rope indicates the youngest brother

私
わたし watashi
シ shi

私 watashi *I*
私立 shiritsu *private*

A farmer is tending to his private crops

These are MY crops

族
ゾク zoku

家族 kazoku *family*
一族 ichizoku *a clan*

Family members travel in the same direction

4

Lesson 23   Hobby 趣味

Trace over the outlines first, then try writing those same characters in the blank boxes. Refer to the guidance on stroke order.

映
- うつ utsu
- エイ ei

映す utsusu — *to reflect or project*
映画 eiga — *movie*

The sun projects a person's shadow on a wall

画
- ガ ga

絵画 kaiga — *painting or picture*
画面 gamen — *screen*

Drawing a picture of a rice paddy on paper

音
- おと oto
- オン on

音 oto — *sound*
音楽 ongaku — *music*

A person stands up and plays music to greet the rising sun

楽
- たの tano
- ガク gaku

楽しい tanoshii — *fun*
楽器 gakki — *musical instrument*

An instrument made of acorns

74

映画音楽写真旅行

写

うつ utsu
シャ sha

写す utsusu — *to copy or trace*
写真 shashin — *picture*

Get the copy from the artist

真

シン shin

真実 shinjitsu — *truth*
真価 shinka — *true value*

Ten eyes examine the artifact to verify its authenticity

4

旅

たび tabi
リョ ryo

旅 tabi — *journey*
旅行する ryokō suru — *to travel or take a trip*

Soldiers are going on a trip

行

い i
コウ kō
ギョウ gyō

行く iku — *to go*
行進 kōshin — *a march or parade*
行列 gyōretsu — *queue or line*

There are two roads to go down

75

Exercise 4

(Answers: p.117)

I   Match the following kanji to their meanings.

円 •   • mother

後 •   • yen

母 •   • minute

弟 •   • younger brother

分 •   • after

II Choose the correct kanji from the right side and write them in the spaces provided.

travel	（　）行	旅・族
free of charge	（　）料	有・無
movie	映（　）	田・画
music	（　）楽	音・暗

Ⅲ　Practice reading the following sentences aloud.

1　私の仕事は、五時三十分に終わります。
2　姉と映画を見に行きました。
3　兄は、写真と音楽が大好きです。
4　旅行は楽しかったですか。
5　午前十時から午後八時まで開いています。
6　私の家族は四人です。
7　音楽を無料でダウンロードできます。
8　弟は時給千円で仕事をしています。
9　一時間後に電話しますね。
10　妹の大学の授業料は高い。

Ⅳ　Write the following words in kanji.

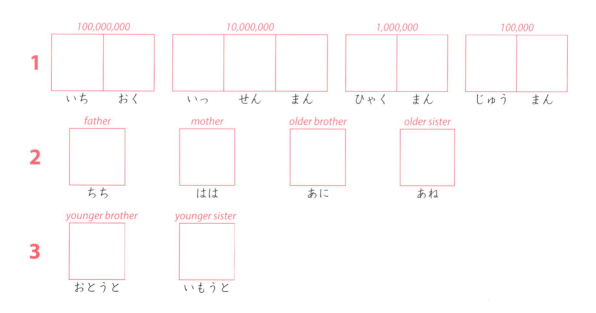

Lesson 24   Food (1)   食(1)

Trace over the outlines first, then try writing those same characters in the blank boxes. Refer to the guidance on stroke order.

食
- た ta
- ショク shoku

食べる　taberu　*to eat*
食事　shokuji　*meal*

Food in a container covered by a lid

牛
- うし ushi
- ギュウ gyū

牛　ushi　*cow*
牛乳　gyūnyū　*cow milk*

The head of a cow

豚
- ぶた buta
- トン ton

豚　buta　*pig*
豚カツ　tonkatsu　*pork cutlet*

A slice of pork next to a pig

鳥
- とり tori
- チョウ chō

鳥　tori　*bird*
野鳥　yachō　*wild bird*

A bird

78

食牛豚鳥魚肉焼乳

魚

さかな sakana
ギョ gyo

魚 sakana *fish*
金魚 kingyo *goldfish*

A fish

肉

ニク niku

牛肉 gyūniku *beef*
豚肉 butaniku *pork*

A cut of meat

焼

や ya
ショウ shō

焼く yaku *to grill or bake*
焼酎 shōchū *distilled liquor*

Grilling something on a stove over a fire

乳

ニュウ nyū

母乳 bonyū *breast milk*
授乳 junyū *lactation*

A breast and a baby with a hat

4

Lesson 25   Food (2)   食(2)

Trace over the outlines first, then try writing those same characters in the blank boxes. Refer to the guidance on stroke order.

野
- の no
- ヤ ya

野原 nohara	*a field or plain*
荒野 kōya	*wilderness or wasteland*

Some grass is growing in the soil of the field next to the vegetable garden

菜
- な na
- サイ sai

菜花 nabana	*rape blossom*
野菜 yasai	*vegetable*

A patch of grass behind a bush with vegetables on it

塩
- しお shio
- エン en

塩 shio	*salt*
塩分 enbun	*salt content*

Mine salt from the ground and put it on a plate

甘
- あま ama
- カン kan

甘い amai	*sweet*
甘味料 kanmiryō	*sweetener*

A boy with a sweet in his mouth

野菜塩甘辛味酢油

辛

- つら　tsura
- から　kara
- シン　shin

辛い　tsurai　*painful or tough*
辛口　karakuchi　*spicy or dry*
香辛料　kōshinryō　*spice*

Getting a tattoo with a needle is painful

味

- あじ　aji
- ミ　mi

味　aji　*taste*
調味料　chōmiryō　*seasoning*

Tasting the new leaf of a plant

酢

- す　su
- サク　saku

酢　su　*vinegar*
酢酸　sakusan　*acetic acid*

Vinegar is made from sake

油

- あぶら　abura
- ユ　yu

油　abura　*oil*
キャノーラ油　kyanōra-yu　*canola oil*

Scooping oil from a container

4

Lesson 26   Drinks 飲

Trace over the outlines first, then try writing those same characters in the blank boxes. Refer to the guidance on stroke order.

飲

の　no
イン　in

| 飲む | nomu | to drink |
| 飲料 | inryō | beverage |

A person drinking sake next to a barrel

茶

ちゃ　cha
サ　sa

| お茶 | o-cha | Japanese tea |
| 茶道 | sadō | tea ceremony |

Use a tool to cut the tea leaves

酒

さけ　sake
さか　saka
シュ　shu

お酒	o-sake	alcohol (refers to all alcoholic drinks)
酒屋	sakaya	liquor store
日本酒	nihonshu	sake (Japanese rice wine)

A sake barrel

酎

チュウ　chū

| 焼酎 | shōchū | a type of distilled liquor |
| 酎ハイ | chūhai | cocktail of shochu with tonic water |

Scooping sake from a barrel

飲茶酒酎紅梅緑割

紅
- べに beni
- コウ kō

口紅 kuchibeni *lipstick*
紅茶 kōcha *black tea (looks red to Japanese)*

Making crafts from red string

梅
- うめ ume
- バイ bai

梅干し umeboshi *dried plum*
白梅 hakubai *white plum flower*

Mother takes care of her plum tree every day

緑
- みどり midori
- リョク ryoku

緑 midori *green*
緑茶 ryokucha *green tea*

Dye the string green by soaking it in water

割
- わ wa
- カツ katsu

割り wari *mixed or diluted with (used for drinks)*
分割 bunkatsu *division or segment*

Use the knife to divide the fish before putting it in your mouth

4

Lesson 27   Time 時(とき)

Trace over the outlines first, then try writing those same characters in the blank boxes. Refer to the guidance on stroke order.

朝
- あさ asa
- チョウ chō

朝 asa — *morning*
朝食 chōshoku — *breakfast*

The sun peeks its head through the grass as the moon sets

昼
- ひる hiru
- チュウ chū

昼間 hiruma — *daytime*
昼食 chūshoku — *lunch*

Daytime ranges from 8 a.m. to 4 p.m.

夕
- ゆう yū
- セキ seki

夕方 yūgata — *early evening (from 4–6 p.m.)*
一朝一夕 itchō isseki — *in a short time; overnight*

The moon often appears in the sky in early evening

夜
- よる yoru
- ヤ ya

夜 yoru — *night*
今夜 kon'ya — *tonight*

A person gazing up at the moon from under a street light

84

朝昼夕夜晩飯今昨

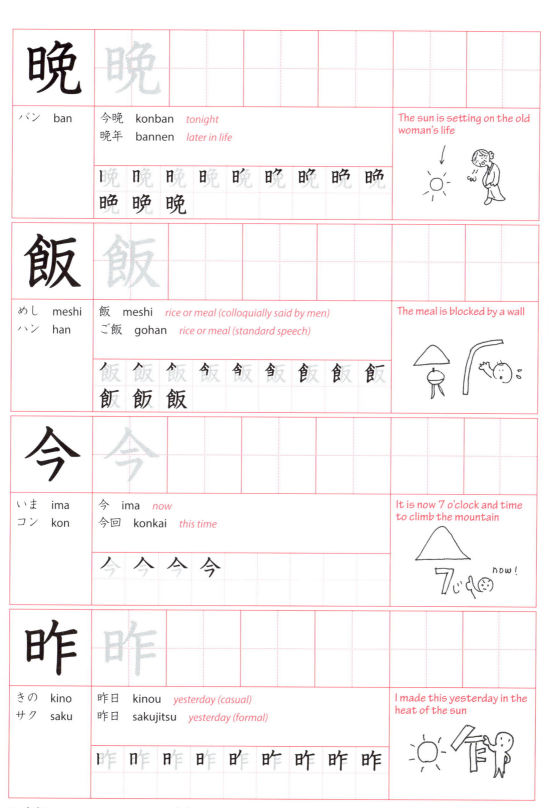

※ 今朝 kesa *this morning*　今年 kotoshi *this year*

Lesson 28 Food (3) 食(3)

Trace over the outlines first, then try writing those same characters in the blank boxes. Refer to the guidance on stroke order.

串

くし　kushi

| 串焼き | kushiyaki | *grilled skewer* |
| 串カツ | kushikatsu | *skewered cutlet* |

A skewer

揚

あ　a

| 揚げる | ageru | *to deep-fry* |
| 揚げ物 | agemono | *fried food* |

Frying some pork skewers under the sun

品

しな　shina
ヒン　hin

| 品物 | shinamono | *goods or merchandise* |
| 五品 | gohin | *five items* |

Three boxes of goods

皿

さら　sara

| 皿 | sara | *plate* |
| 大皿 | ōzara | *large plate or platter* |

A plate with food on it

串揚品皿盛物放題

盛
- も mo
- セイ sei

大盛り　ōmori　*large serving*
盛大　seidai　*grand or magnificent (in scale)*

Putting many things on a plate

物
- もの mono
- ブツ butsu

食べ物　tabemono　*food*
動物　dōbutsu　*animal*

The head of a cow and the side profile of another animal

放
- はな hana
- ホウ hō

放す　hanasu　*to release or let go*
放送　hōsō　*broadcast*

Release the weapons in that direction

題
- ダイ dai

食べ放題　tabehōdai　*all you can eat*
題名　daimei　*title*

Grill as much shellfish as you want under the sun

4

Exercise 5

(Answers: p.118)

I   Match the following kanji to their meanings.

緑　•　　　　　•　deep-fried

塩　•　　　　　•　salt

酒　•　　　　　•　green

今　•　　　　　•　alcohol

揚　•　　　　　•　now

II   Choose the correct kanji from the right side and write them in the spaces provided.

beef	（　）肉	牛・午
tonight	今（　）	朝・晩
goods	品（　）	物・揚
black tea	（　）茶	緑・紅
drinks	（　）物	食・飲

Ⅲ　Practice reading the following sentences aloud.

1　晩ご飯は牛肉と野菜の炒(いた)め物にしましょう。
2　父は焼酎の梅割りと焼き鳥が大好きなんですよ。
3　天ぷらの盛り合わせは、八百円です。
4　この串カツは油っぽいですね。
5　カレーには甘口と辛口があります。
6　ここの焼肉は食べ放題ですか。
7　酢の物って何ですか。
8　小さいお皿をもらえますか。
9　私は豚肉が苦(にが)手なんです。
10　焼き魚定食をお願いします。

Ⅳ　Write the following words in kanji.

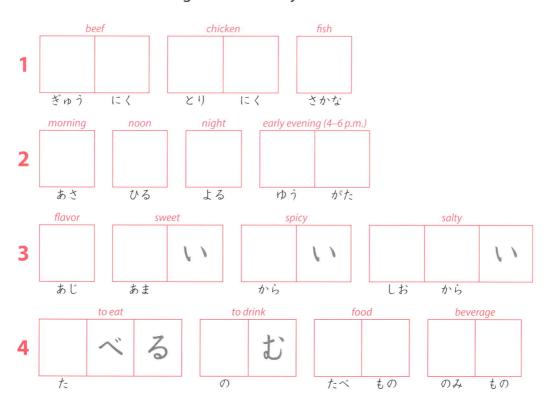

Lesson 29 Buildings (1) 建物(1)

たてもの

Trace over the outlines first, then try writing those same characters in the blank boxes. Refer to the guidance on stroke order.

館

- やかた yakata
- カン kan

館 yakata — *mansion*
美術館 bijutsukan — *art museum*

Many people are dining inside the mansion

堂

- ドウ dō

本堂 hondō — *main building of a temple*
食堂 shokudō — *cafeteria*

A deity reaches down to receive the temple's offering

場

- ば ba
- ジョウ jō

職場 shokuba — *workplace*
工場 kōjō — *factory*

There is a cross at the place where the sun shines on a pig

会

- あ a
- カイ kai

会う au — *to meet*
会場 kaijō — *venue*

The boy jumps for joy because he can meet his favorite singer at the venue

館堂場会店屋局来

店

みせ mise テン ten	店 mise *shop or store* 本店 honten *main store*

A person selling goods in a shop

屋

や ya オク oku	本屋 hon'ya *bookstore* 屋上 okujō *rooftop*

A man sells dirt from his house

局

キョク kyoku	郵便局 yūbinkyoku *post office* 薬局 yakkyoku *pharmacy*

The post office building is shaped like a mailbox with its flag up

来

く ku き ki こ ko ライ rai	来る kuru *to come* 来た kita *came* 来られる korareru *to be able to come* 来年 rainen *next year*

The rye flowers are blooming so harvest time has come

4

Lesson 30   Buildings (2)   建物(2)

Trace over the outlines first, then try writing those same characters in the blank boxes. Refer to the guidance on stroke order.

神

- かみ　kami
- ジン　jin

神様　kamisama　*god*
雷神　raijin　*god of thunder*

God threw lightning at the rice paddy so the scared farmers put an offering on the altar nearby

宮

- みや　miya
- グウ　gū
- キュウ　kyū

お宮参り　o-miyamairi　*taking a newborn to a shrine to pray*
神宮　jingū　*imperial Shinto shrine*
宮殿　kyūden　*palace*

The palace has two big rooms

銀

- ギン　gin

銀行　ginkō　*bank*
金銀　kingin　*gold and silver*

A gold coin next to a silver trophy

社

- やしろ　yashiro
- シャ　sha
- ジャ　ja

社　yashiro　*a shrine building*
会社　kaisha　*company*
神社　jinja　*shrine*

Put the clay offering on the altar

92

神宮銀社役病医院

役

ヤク　yaku
エキ　eki

市役所　shiyakusho　*city hall*
兵役　heieki　*military service*

A soldier with a hat and two swords heads down the road to fulfill his duty

病

やまい　yamai
ビョウ　byō

病　yamai　*disease (used in literature)*
病気　byōki　*disease or illness*

Looking in on a sick person through a small window

医

イ　i

医者　isha　*doctor*
医学　igaku　*medical science*

The doctor practices medicine in his square office

院

イン　in

医院　iin　*doctor's office*
入院　nyūin　*hospitalization*

Go up the stairs to enter the hospital building

4

93

Lesson 31 Transportation 交通(こうつう)

Trace over the outlines first, then try writing those same characters in the blank boxes. Refer to the guidance on stroke order.

乗

の no
ジョウ jō

乗る　noru　*to ride on*
乗車する　jōsha suru　*to get on a train, bus, taxi*

A person riding on a gondola

降

お o
コウ kō

降りる　oriru　*to get off*
降下する　kōka suru　*to descend*

A man with a crutch trying to descend stairs

駅

エキ eki

東京駅　Tōkyō Eki　*Tokyo Station*
駅前　ekimae　*in front of a station*

Horses are hitched to posts outside the station

始

はじ haji
シ shi

始める　hajimeru　*to start (something)*
始発　shihatsu　*the first train (of the day)*

A woman kneels down to start the ceremony

乗降駅始発着往復

発

ハツ　hatsu

| 発車 | hassha | *departure* |
| 発見 | hakken | *discovery* |

Let's depart from the house that has many flags

着

き　ki
つ　tsu
チャク　chaku

着る	kiru	*to wear*
着く	tsuku	*to arrive*
到着	tōchaku	*arrival*

The king arrived wearing a gorgeous striped robe and a cloak

往

オウ　ō

| 往復 | ōfuku | *round-trip* |
| 往路 | ōro | *the outbound leg of a trip* |

Making a round-trip to the master's house

復

フク　fuku

| 復路 | fukuro | *return trip* |
| 復学 | fukugaku | *re-enroll in school* |

The Sun walks down the road on his return trip home

4

Lesson 32   Movement 動

Trace over the outlines first, then try writing those same characters in the blank boxes. Refer to the guidance on stroke order.

自
- シ shi
- ジ ji

自然 shizen — *nature or natural*
自分 jibun — *oneself*

Japanese point at their noses to indicate themselves

動
- うご ugo
- ドウ dō

動かす ugokasu — *to move (something)*
自動 jidō — *automatic*

The strong worker moves a heavy object to the ground

車
- くるま kuruma
- シャ sha

車 kuruma — *car*
自動車 jidōsha — *automobile*

A car

工
- コウ kō
- ク ku

工事 kōji — *construction*
大工 daiku — *carpenter*

A wooden structure built by a carpenter

96

自動車工歩折通訳

歩

| あるaru | 歩く | aruku | to walk |
| ホ ho | 歩道 | hodō | sidewalk |

A set of footprints

折

| お o | 折る | oru | to break |
| セツ setsu | 左折 | sasetsu | left turn |

Break a stick with an axe

通

| とお tō | 通る | tōru | to pass |
| ツウ tsū | 通行人 | tsūkōnin | passer-by |

Wind passing through a bell

転

| ころ koro | 転がす | korogasu | to roll (something) |
| テン ten | 運転 | unten | to drive or operate |

A woman operating the two rollers of a machine

4

97

Lesson 33 Seasons 季節(きせつ)

Trace over the outlines first, then try writing those same characters in the blank boxes. Refer to the guidance on stroke order.

春

はる　haru
シュン　shun

春　haru　*spring*
春分の日　shunbun no hi　*spring equinox*

The bright sun of spring helps plants grow tall

夏

なつ　natsu
カ　ka

夏　natsu　*summer*
夏期講座　kaki kōza　*summer course*

A person feels dizzy from the summer heat

秋

あき　aki
シュウ　shū

秋　aki　*autumn*
晩秋　banshū　*late fall*

Leaves turn fiery colors in autumn

冬

ふゆ　fuyu
トウ　tō

冬　fuyu　*winter*
冬至　tōji　*winter solstice*

People enjoy skiing in the winter

春夏秋冬季節暑寒

季

キ　ki

| 季節 | kisetsu | *season* |
| 夏季 | kaki | *summer season* |

The child enjoys watching the plants change with the seasons

節

ふし　fushi
セツ　setsu

| 節目 | fushime | *a joint or knot* |
| 節分 | setsubun | *Japanese celebration marking the end of winter* |

Snakes do "knot" eat bamboo—they prefer apples

4

暑

あつ　atsu
ショ　sho

| 暑い | atsui | *hot* |
| 残暑 | zansho | *late summer heat* |

Baking clay is fast under two hot suns

寒

さむ　samu
カン　kan

| 寒い | samui | *cold* |
| 大寒 | daikan | *the coldest time of year* |

You have to break icicles off the roof in cold weather

Exercise 6

(Answers: p.119)

Ⅰ Match the following kanji to their meanings.

店　•　　　　　•　walk

神　•　　　　　•　station

駅　•　　　　　•　winter

歩　•　　　　　•　store

冬　•　　　　　•　god

Ⅱ Choose the correct kanji from the right side and write them in the spaces provided.

place	場（　）	所・近
bank	（　）行	金・銀
round-trip	往（　）	復・複
automatic	（　）動	自・目
season	季（　）	飲・節

Ⅲ　Practice reading the following sentences aloud.

1　車で病院に行きます。
2　神社まで歩きましょう。
3　どの駅で降りればいいですか。
4　東京発・大阪行きの電車に乗ってください。
5　私の好きな季節は夏です。
6　北海道の冬は寒いですね。
7　市役所はどこですか。
8　医者に病気を治^{なお}してもらいました。
9　自動車工場ではたらいています。
10　そこは工事中なので、右折してください。

Ⅳ　Write the following words in kanji.

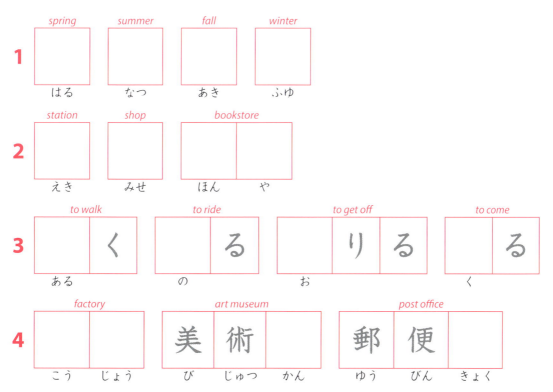

第五章
日常生活で使われる漢字（読みだけ）

Lesson 34 — Store Signs 店の看板

open

closed (preparing to open)

closed (as scheduled)

operating hours

We are closed today.

closed (for some special reason)

Lesson 35 Information 案内(あんない)

案内 *an nai* — Information

開館時間 *kai kan ji kan* — opening time	午前9時30分 *go zen ku ji san ju ppun* — 9:30 a.m.
閉館時間 *hei kan ji kan* — closing time	午後5時30分（入館は5時まで） *go go go ji san ju ppun, nyū kan wa go ji ma de* — 5:30 p.m. (entry permitted until 5 o'clock)
休館日 *kyū kan bi* — closed on (days)	毎週月曜日、年末年始 *mai shū getsu yō bi, nenmatsu nen shi* — every Monday, the New Year's holiday period
	（12月28日〜1月3日） *jū ni gatsu nijū hachi nichi – ichi gatsu mi kka* — (December 28 through January 3)

料金 *ryō kin* — fee

一般 *i ppan* — general admission	700円 *nana hyaku en* — 700 yen
大学・高校 *dai gaku / kō kō* — university or high-school student	500円 *go hyaku en* — 500 yen
中学生以下 *chū gaku sei i ka* — middle-school student or younger	無料 *mu ryō* — free

Entrance fees for children are usually determined by school grade rather than age.

Lesson 36 Meal Tickets 食券(しょっけん)

食券 (sho kken) — meal ticket
硬貨 (kō ka) — coin
紙幣 (shi hei) — bill (paper money)
天丼 (ten don) — tempura on rice
牛丼 (gyū don) — beef on rice
親子丼 (oya ko don) — chicken and egg on rice
餃子 (gyō za) — pan-fried dumplings
焼き魚定食 (ya ki zakana tei shoku) — grilled-fish set meal
豚カツ定食 (ton ka tsu tei shoku) — pork-cutlet set meal
券取り出し口 (ken to ri da shi guchi) — ticket dispensing slot
返却口 (hen kyaku guchi) — change slot
水 (mizu) — water

Lesson 37   Menu お品書き(しなが)

o-shina ga ki	
お品書き *Menu*	

zen sai saki zuke **前菜・先付** *appetizer*	te ri ya ki **照り焼き** *teriyaki*
ya ki mono **焼き物** *grilled dish*	ya ki zakana **焼き魚** *grilled fish*
a ge mono **揚げ物** *deep-fried dish*	ten pu ra **天ぷら** *tempura*
ko bachi **小鉢** *small dish*	sashi mi **刺身** *raw sliced fish*
tei shoku **定食** *set meal*	mi so shiru **味噌汁** *miso soup*
tei ban **定番** *classic or standard*	men **麺** *noodles*
donburi **丼** *bowl of rice with a topping*	go han **御飯** *rice*
mo ri a wa se **盛り合わせ** *combination platter*	nabe **鍋** *hot pot dish*
tō fu **豆腐** *tofu*	

5

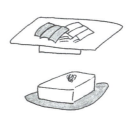

Lesson 38   Station 駅(えき)

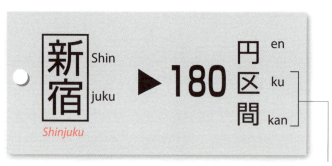

地下鉄 (chi ka tetsu) — subway
JR線 (sen) — JR line
普通 (fu tsū) — local
快速 (kai soku) — rapid-service

新宿 (Shinjuku) ▶ 180円 区間 (en / ku kan)
section of track between two locations

乗車券 (jō sha ken) — passenger ticket
東京都区内 (Tō kyō to ku nai) within Tokyo ➡ 名古屋市内 (Na go ya shi nai) within Nagoya
12月31日から3日間有効 (jūni gatsu sanjūichi nichi ka ra mikka kan yū ko) — valid for three days starting on December 31
¥6090

新幹線特急券 (shin kan sen to kkyū ken) — express ticket for bullet train
東京 (Tō kyō) ➡ 名古屋 (Na go ya)
12月31日   7号車 15番C席 (nana gō sha jū go ban seki) — car 7 seat 15-C
¥4890

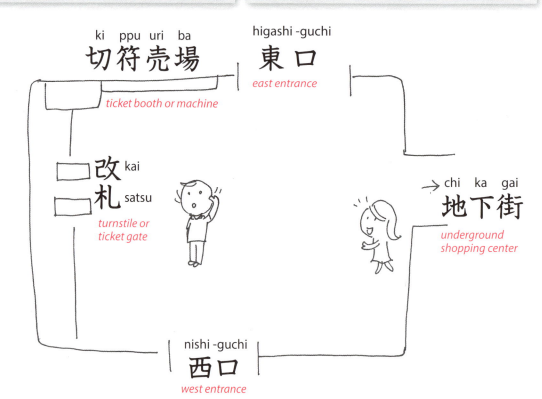

切符売場 (ki ppu uri ba) — ticket booth or machine
東口 (higashi-guchi) — east entrance
改札 (kai satsu) — turnstile or ticket gate
地下街 (chi ka gai) — underground shopping center
西口 (nishi-guchi) — west entrance

Lesson 39　Parking Lot 駐車場

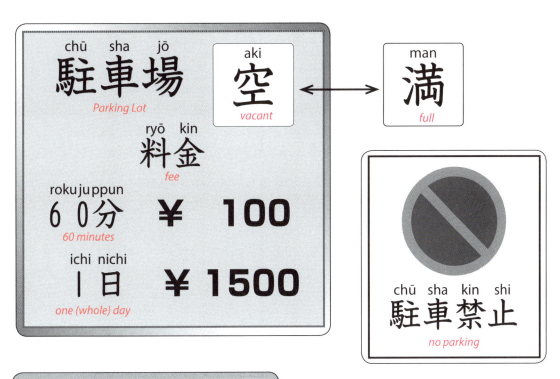

Lesson 40   Remote Control リモコン

Japanese "air conditioners" can blow out heat too!

エアコン (e a ko n) Air Conditioner

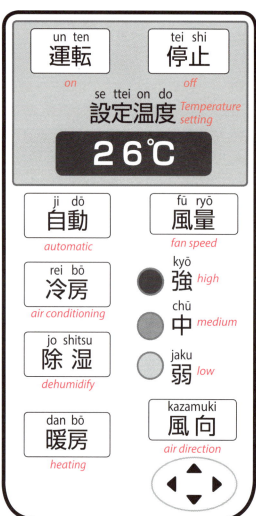

- 運転 (un ten) — on
- 停止 (tei shi) — off
- 設定温度 (se ttei on do) — Temperature setting
- 26℃
- 自動 (ji dō) — automatic
- 風量 (fū ryō) — fan speed
- 冷房 (rei bō) — air conditioning
- 強 (kyō) — high
- 中 (chū) — medium
- 除湿 (jo shitsu) — dehumidify
- 弱 (jaku) — low
- 暖房 (dan bō) — heating
- 風向 (kazamuki) — air direction

TV リモコン (terebi ri mo ko n) TV Remote

- 入力切替 (nyū ryoku kiri kae) — input
- 電源 (den gen) — power
- 音量 (on ryō) — volume
- 選局 (sen kyoku) — channel select
- 再生 (sai sei) — play
- 停止 (tei shi) — stop
- 録画 (roku ga) — record
- 一時停止 (ichi ji tei shi) — pause

Lesson 41 Rice Cooker 炊飯器

sui han ・ ta ku 炊飯・炊く	start (cooking)
ho on 保温	keep warm
tori keshi 取消	clear/cancel
kyū soku 急速	quick
yo yaku 予約	set timer
haku mai 白米	white rice
gen mai 玄米	brown rice
ta ki ko mi 炊き込み	mixed rice (added vegetables etc.)

Microwave 電子レンジ

ji dō 自動	automatic
tori keshi 取消	clear/cancel
on do 温度	temperature
atata me 温め	heat
kai tō 解凍	defrost

Lesson 42

Washing Machine 洗濯機(せんたくき)

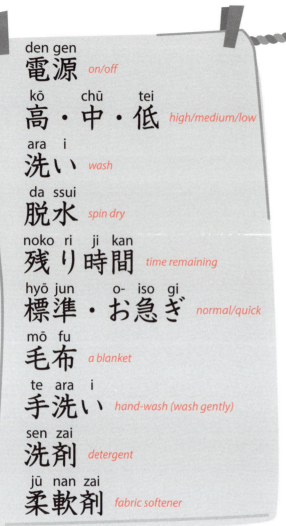

den gen
電源 — on/off

kō chū tei
高・中・低 — high/medium/low

ara i
洗い — wash

da ssui
脱水 — spin dry

noko ri ji kan
残り時間 — time remaining

hyō jun　o- iso gi
標準・お急ぎ — normal/quick

mō fu
毛布 — a blanket

te ara i
手洗い — hand-wash (wash gently)

sen zai
洗剤 — detergent

jū nan zai
柔軟剤 — fabric softener

Restroom トイレ

wa shiki　yō shiki
和式・洋式 — Japanese-style / Western-style

naga su
流す — flush

ji dō sui sen
自動水洗 — automatic flushing system

ji dō da sshū
自動脱臭 — automatic deodorizer

oto hime
音姫 — flushing-sound system

dan bō ben za
暖房便座 — heated seat

setsu den
節電 — energy-saving mode

yobi dashi
呼出 — emergency call

112

Lesson 43 Hospital/Clinic 病院(びょういん)

診察券 (shin satsu ken) — patient ID card
様 (sama) — Mr. / Mrs.
No.

	月 getsu Mon	火 ka Tue	水 sui Wed	木 moku Thu	金 kin Fri	土 do Sat
午前 go zen (morning) 9〜12	○	○	○	○	○	○
午後 go go (afternoon) 4〜6	○	○	○	/	○	/

休診日 (kyū shin bi) closed : 日曜 (nichi yō) Sun ・ 祝日 (shuku jitsu) Holidays

問診票 (mon shin hyō) — medical questionnaire

症状 (shō jō) — symptoms

痛み (ita mi) — pain

左 (hidari) left   右 (migi) right

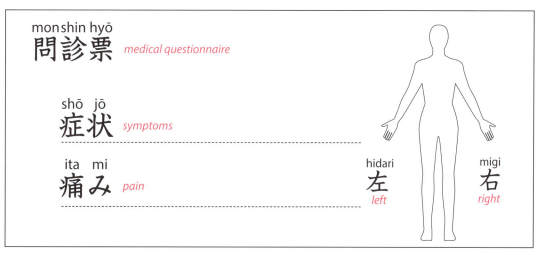

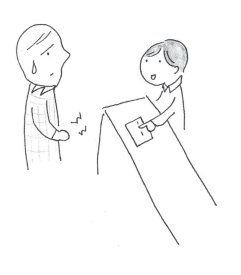

内用薬 (nai yō yaku) — oral medication

一日 (ichi nichi) 2回 (ni kai) 五日分 (itsu ka bun)
twice a day for five days

朝・昼・夕 (asa・hiru・yū) morning/noon/evening

食前 (shoku zen) before meals
食後 (shoku go) after meals

錠剤 (jō zai) pill or tablet ／ 一錠 (ichi jō) one pill or tablet

粉薬 (konagusuri) powder medication ／ 一包 (i ppō) one pack

5

Lesson 44   School 学校 (がっこう)

ji kan wari
時間割
schedule

shuku dai
宿題
homework

shu sseki
出席
attendance

ke sseki
欠席
absence

han nichi
半日
half-day

ka tei hō mon
家庭訪問
home visit (by a teacher)

ren raku chō
連絡帳
notebook for parent-teacher communication

mo chi mono
持ち物
things to bring with you

tai sō fuku
体操服
gym clothes

uwa ba ki
上履き
indoor shoes

sui tō
水筒
thermos bottle

ben tō
弁当
packed lunch

gyō ji
行事
event or function

ju gyō san kan
授業参観
class observation day (for parents)

en soku
遠足
field trip

un dō kai
運動会
sports day

ha ppyō kai
発表会
recital

nyū gaku shiki
入学式
school entrance ceremony

sotsu gyō shiki
卒業式
school graduation ceremony

shi gyō shiki
始業式
opening ceremony (of a school term)

shū gyō shiki
終業式
closing ceremony (of a school term)

ho go sha
保護者
parent or guardian

kon dan kai
懇談会
parent-teacher meeting

Lesson 45　　Ordering 注文(ちゅうもん)

☐ 買い物かご ka i mono ka go *cart*
☐ 欲しい物リスト ho shi i mono ri su to *wish list*
☐ お気に入り o- ki ni i ri *favorites*

☐ 購入 kō nyū *purchase*
☐ 数量 sū ryō *quantity*
☐ 削除 saku jo *delete*
送料無料 sō ryō mu ryō *free shipping*
発送 ha ssō *shipped*

5

購入手続き kō nyū te tsuzu ki *ordering process*
お届け先住所 o- todo ke saki jū sho *shipping address*
お支払方法 o- shi harai hō hō *payment method*
・代引き dai bi ki *collect on delivery* ☐
・着払い chaku bara i *cash on delivery* ☐

ご不在連絡票 go- fu zai ren raku hyō
notice of attempted delivery

様 sama *Mr. / Mrs.*

再配達 sai hai tatsu *redelivery*

配達ご希望日 hai ta tsu ki bō bi *requested delivery date*

Answers

Exercise 1 (p.36)

I 金 = gold　生 = raw　休 = rest　好 = like　雨 = rain

II 入口　右手　禁煙　見る

III
1 いちがつ ついたちは やすみです。 *January 1st is a holiday.*
2 みずを にはい おねがいします。 *Two glasses of water, please.*
3 あの おおきいひとは、やまださんです。 *That big guy is Mr. Yamada.*
4 この おとこのこは、その おんなのこが すきです。 *This boy likes that girl.*
5 もりの なかは くらいです。 *It is dark inside the forest.*
6 あしたの てんきは、はれでしょう。 *Tomorrow's weather will be sunny.*
7 ひだりてを みてください。 *Please look at the left-hand side.*
8 ここは、たちいりきんしです。 *Entering here is forbidden.*
9 にほんじんは、めが ちいさいです。 *Japanese people have small eyes.*
10 じょせいの こころは ふくざつです。 *The heart of a woman is complicated.*

IV
1 月　火　水　木　金　土
2 雨　晴れ　雪　台風
3 一人　二人　三人　四人　五人
4 四月四日　九月二十日

Exercise 2 (p.54)

I 海 = sea　客 = guest　読 = read　終 = finish　何 = what

II 安心　日記　一回　定価

III
1 いっしゅうかんに にかい ジムに いきます。 *I go to the gym twice a week.*
2 ちゅうい してください。 *You should be careful.*
3 みずうみは いけより おおきいです。 *Lakes are bigger than ponds.*
4 この かみに ちずを かきましょうか。 *Shall I draw a map on this piece of paper?*
5 もんを あけてください。 *Please open the gate.*
6 けっこんしています。 *I'm married.*
7 その じょうだんは なんかいも ききましたよ。 *I've heard that joke many times.*
8 ここの ちかくに すんでいます。 *I live near here.*
9 みちに まよいました。 *I am lost.*
10 ようちえんは しまっています。 *The kindergarten is closed.*

IV
1 言う　話す　聞く　訳す
2 糸　綿　絹　結ぶ
3 送る　近い　道　一週間
4 みそ汁　汗　注ぐ　泣く

Exercise 3 (p.66)

I 町 = town   南 = south   高 = high   先 = ahead   区 = ward

II 東京　授業　学校　住所

III
1. なんさいですか。 *How old are you?*
2. がっこうの じゅぎょうは むずかしいです。 *My classes at school are difficult.*
3. わたしは、こうこうに ねんせいです。 *I'm in my second year of high school.*
4. すきな きょうかは なんですか。 *What is your favorite subject?*
5. しめい、しょくぎょう、でんわばんごうを きにゅうする。
   Fill in your name, occupation, and phone number.
6. おおさかふは かんさいちほうに あります。 *Osaka is in the Kansai region.*
7. とうきょうとは かんとうちほうに あります。 *Tokyo is in the Kanto region.*
8. きょうとに じゅうねん すんでいます。 *I've been living in Kyoto for ten years.*
9. アメリカの しゅうで、テキサスしゅうは にばんめに おおきいです。
   Texas is the second largest state in America.
10. にほんには、けんが あります。 *Japan has prefectures.*

IV
1. 住所　電話番号
2. 方角　北　南　東　西
3. 小学校　中学校　高校

Exercise 4 (p.76)

I 円 = yen   後 = after   母 = mother   弟 = younger brother   分 = minute

II 旅行　無料　映画　音楽

III
1. わたしの しごとは、ごじさんじゅっぷんに おわります。 *My job finishes at 5:30.*
2. あねと えいがを みにいきました。 *I went to see a movie with my older sister.*
3. あには、しゃしんと おんがくが だいすきです。
   My older brother really likes photography and music.
4. りょこうは たのしかったですか。 *Did you have fun on your trip?*
5. ごぜんじゅうじから ごごはちじまで あいています。 *They are open from 10 a.m. to 8 p.m.*
6. わたしの かぞくは よにんです。 *We are a family of four.*
7. おんがくを むりょうで だうんろーどできます。 *You can download the music for free.*
8. おとうとは じきゅうせんえんで しごとを しています。
   My younger brother works for 1,000 yen an hour.
9. いちじかんごに でんわしますね。 *I'll call you in one hour.*
10. いもうとの だいがくの じゅぎょうりょうは たかい。
    My younger sister's college tuition is expensive.

IV
1. 一億　一千万　百万　十万
2. 父　母　兄　姉
3. 弟　妹

117

Answers

Exercise 5 (p.88)

Ⅰ　緑 = green　塩 = salt　酒 = alcohol　今 = now　揚 = deep-fried

Ⅱ　牛肉　今晩　品物　紅茶　飲物

Ⅲ　1　ばんごはんは ぎゅうにくと やさいの いためものに しましょう。
　　　Let's stir-fry some beef and vegetables for dinner.
　　2　ちちは、しょうちゅうの うめわりと やきとりが だいすきなんですよ。
　　　My father loves plum liquor and yakitori (grilled-chicken skewers).
　　3　てんぷらの もりあわせは、はっぴゃくえんです。 *An order of assorted tempura costs 800 yen.*
　　4　この くしカツは あぶらっぽいですね。 *This pork-cutlet skewer is oily.*
　　5　カレーには あまくちと からくちが あります。 *There are both sweet and spicy types of curry.*
　　6　ここの やきにくは たべほうだい ですか。 *Is the yakiniku (barbecued meat) here all-you-can-eat?*
　　7　すのものって なんですか。 *What is "su no mono"?*
　　8　ちいさい おさらを もらえますか。 *May I have a small plate?*
　　9　わたしは ぶたにくが にがて なんです。 *I'm not a big fan of pork.*
　　10　やきざかなていしょくを おねがいします。 *I'll have the grilled-fish set please.*

Ⅳ　1　牛肉　鳥肉　魚
　　2　朝　昼　夜　夕方
　　3　味　甘い　辛い　塩辛い
　　4　食べる　飲む　食べ物　飲み物

Exercise 6 (p.100)

Ⅰ　店 = store　神 = god　駅 = station　歩 = walk　冬 = winter

Ⅱ　場所　銀行　往復　自動　季節

Ⅲ　1　くるまで びょういんに いきます。 *I'll drive to the hospital.*
　　2　じんじゃまで あるきましょう。 *Let's walk to the shrine.*
　　3　どのえきで おりれば いいですか。 *Which station should I get off at?*
　　4　とうきょうはつ・おおさかいきの でんしゃに のってください。
　　　Take the train that runs from Tokyo to Osaka.
　　5　わたしの すきな きせつは なつです。 *My favorite season is summer.*
　　6　ほっかいどうの ふゆは さむいですね。 *Winters in Hokkaido are cold.*
　　7　しやくしょは どこですか。 *Where is city hall?*
　　8　いしゃに びょうきを なおしてもらいました。 *I had a doctor treat my illness.*
　　9　じどうしゃ こうじょうで はたらいています。 *I'm working in an automobile factory.*
　　10　そこは こうじちゅうなので、うせつしてください
　　　There's construction going on over there, so turn right please.

Ⅳ　1　春　夏　秋　冬
　　2　駅　店　本屋
　　3　歩く　乗る　降りる　来る
　　4　工場　美術館　郵便局

Index

数字(すうじ)	一 二 三 四 五	p. 20
	六 七 八 九 十	p. 21
曜日(ようび)	月 火 水 木	p. 22
	金 土 日 曜	p. 23
自然(しぜん)	山 川 田 井	p. 24
	生 竹 羽 立	p. 25
大きさ(おおきさ)記号(きごう)	大 中 小 人	p. 26
	上 下 休 入	p. 27
性別(せいべつ)特性(とくせい)	力 子 女 男	p. 28
	好 心 性 学	p. 29
体(からだ)左右(さゆう)	目 口 耳 出	p. 30
	手 見 右 左	p. 31
組み合わせた漢字(くみあわせたかんじ)	林 森 明 暗	p. 32
	禁 止 煙 災	p. 33
天気(てんき)	天 気 晴 温	p. 34
	雨 雪 風 台	p. 35
さんずい	汁 海 池 湖	p. 40
	泣 注 汗 活	p. 41
うかんむり	家 安 客 室	p. 42
	害 守 容 定	p. 43
ごんべん	言 話 語 訳	p. 44
	談 読 記 計	p. 45

いとへん	糸 綿 絹 結	p. 46
	紙 約 終 給	p. 47
にんべん	使 作 何 住	p. 48
	価 値 代 付	p. 49
しんにょう	道 近 遠 迷	p. 50
	送 迎 返 週	p. 51
門(もん)がまえ	門 開 閉 聞	p. 52
国(くに)がまえ	国 図 回 園	p. 53
情報(じょうほう)	氏 名 才 所	p. 58
	電 番 号 職	p. 59
住所(じゅうしょ)	県 市 区 町	p. 60
	州 京 府 都	p. 61
方角(ほうがく)	東 西 南 北	p. 62
	関 地 方 角	p. 63
学校(がっこう)	校 先 年 高	p. 64
	教 科 授 業	p. 65
時間(じかん)	午 前 後 時	p. 68
	間 分 仕 事	p. 69
お金(かね)	円 料 無 有	p. 70
	億 万 千 百	p. 71
家族(かぞく)	母 父 兄 姉	p. 72
	妹 弟 私 族	p. 73

趣味(しゅみ)	映 画 音 楽	p. 74
	写 真 旅 行	p. 75
食(しょく)	食 牛 豚 烏	p. 78
	魚 肉 焼 乳	p. 79
	野 菜 塩 甘	p. 80
	辛 味 酢 油	p. 81
	串 揚 品 皿	p. 86
	盛 物 放 題	p. 87
飲(いん)	飲 茶 酒 酎	p. 82
	紅 梅 緑 割	p. 83
時(とき)	朝 昼 夕 夜	p. 84
	晩 飯 今 昨	p. 85
建物(たてもの)	館 堂 場 会	p. 90
	店 屋 局 来	p. 91
	神 宮 銀 社	p. 92
	役 病 医 院	p. 93
交通(こうつう)	乗 降 駅 始	p. 94
	発 着 往 復	p. 95
動(どう)	自 動 車 工	p. 96
	歩 折 通 転	p. 97
季節(きせつ)	春 夏 秋 冬	p. 98
	季 節 暑 寒	p. 99

日常生活(にちじょうせいかつ)で使(つか)われる漢字(かんじ)

店(みせ)の看板(かんばん)	営業中 準備中 定休日 営業時間 本日 終了 臨時休業	p. 104
案内(あんない)	開館時間 閉館時間 入館 休館日 毎週月曜日 年末年始 料金 一般 大学 高校 中学生以下 無料	p. 105
食券(しょっけん)	硬貨 紙幣 天丼 牛丼 親子丼 餃子 焼き魚定食 豚カツ定食 券取り出し口 返却口 水	p. 106
お品書(しなが)き	前菜 先付 焼き物 揚げ物 小鉢 定食 定番 丼 盛り合わせ 豆腐 照り焼き 焼き魚 天ぷら 刺身 味噌汁 麺 御飯 鍋	p. 107
駅(えき)	新宿 180円区間 地下鉄 JR線 普通 快速 乗車券 東京都区内 名古屋市内 3日間有効 新幹線特急券 東京 名古屋 7号車15番C席 切符売場 東口 改札 地下街 西口	p. 108
駐車場(ちゅうしゃじょう)	空 満 料金 駐車禁止 お客様駐車場 2時間無料 月極駐車場 駐車券 精算機	p. 109
リモコン	運転 停止 設定温度 自動 冷房 除湿 暖房 風量 強 中 弱 風向 入力切替 電源 音量 選局 再生 停止 録画 一時停止	p. 110
炊飯器(すいはんき)	炊飯 炊く 保温 取消 急速 予約 白米 玄米 炊き込み	p. 111
電子(でんし)レンジ	自動 取消 温度 温め 解凍	p. 111
洗濯機(せんたくき)	電源 高 中 低 洗い 脱水 残り時間 標準 お急ぎ 毛布 手洗い 洗剤 柔軟剤	p. 112
トイレ	和式 洋式 流す 自動水洗 自動脱臭 音姫 暖房便座 節電 呼出	p. 112
病院(びょういん)	診察券 様 休診日 日曜 祝日 問診票 症状 痛み 内用薬 一日2回 五日分 食前 食後 錠剤 一錠 粉薬 一包	p. 113
学校(がっこう)	宿題 時間割 出席 欠席 半日 家庭訪問 連絡帳 持ち物 体操服 上履き 水筒 弁当 保護者 懇談会 行事 授業参観 遠足 運動会 発表会 入学式 卒業式 始業式 終業式	p. 114
注文(ちゅうもん)	買い物かご 欲しい物リスト お気に入り 購入 数量 削除 送料無料 発送 購入手続き お届け先住所 お支払方法 代引き 着払い ご不在連絡票 再配達 配達ご希望日	p. 115

EASY AND FUN
KANJI

2017年 9月 1日 第1刷発行
2025年 7月 6日 第4刷発行

著者　　小川　清美
発行者　賀川　洋
発行所　IBCパブリッシング株式会社
　　　　〒162-0804 東京都新宿区中里町29番3号 菱秀神楽坂ビル
　　　　Tel. 03-3513-4511　Fax. 03-3513-4512
　　　　www.ibcpub.co.jp

印刷所　中央精版印刷株式会社

© 小川清美 2017
Printed in Japan

落丁本・乱丁本は、小社宛にお送りください。送料小社負担にてお取り替えいたします。
本書の無断複写（コピー）は著作権法上での例外を除き禁じられています。

ISBN978-4-7946-0501-6